*Sociology and Contemporary Education*

\* \*

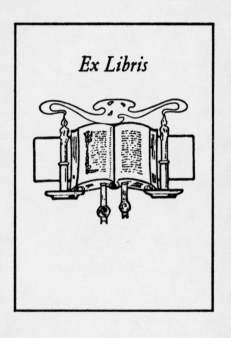

*Ex Libris*

# SOCIOLOGY AND CONTEMPORARY EDUCATION

\* \*

*Robert Bierstedt*
NEW YORK UNIVERSITY

*Marvin Bressler*
PRINCETON UNIVERSITY

*Ely Chinoy*
SMITH COLLEGE

*Robert A. Nisbet*
UNIVERSITY OF CALIFORNIA, RIVERSIDE

*Charles H. Page*
PRINCETON UNIVERSITY

Edited by Charles H. Page
*Foreword by David Riesman*

RANDOM HOUSE
*New York*

# *Foreword*

In his essay, "Popular Sociology," Ely Chinoy observes that Vance Packard, E. C. Spectorsky, Russell Lynes, and other practitioners in this genre emphasize status strivings and styles of life to the almost total neglect of economic and political fissures in the class structure of the United States. In this way, Chinoy claims, they reflect, despite the apparent sharpness of their critiques, both the affluence that has overtaken the great middle majority of Americans and the relative muting of class consciousness or "end of ideology" in post-War America. It is, I would think, at least in part, a reflection of similar tendencies that what might be termed the newer social sciences of sociology, cultural anthropology, and the more "social" branches of psychology have tended both inside and outside the academy to rise in esteem in comparison with the older social sciences of history, government (as distinguished from more behavioristic political science), experimental and general psychology, and particularly economics. Many undergraduates of either ambitious or reformist bent, or belonging to that rare minority motivated by idle curiosity who might in the 1930's have studied economics, now study sociology either in departments of that name or in general education programs keyed to these newer social sciences. (Directly in Charles Page's case and indirectly in Marvin Bressler's chapter, there is reference to the large group of women who now are recruited into the study of sociology or into the audience for popular sociology, and what the attitudes are toward this constituency among professors of sociology who are, with few exceptions, men. Both in the great state and private universities of the modern frontier and in the centers of mass education, to use the categories Charles Page presents in Chapter 1, there has been, in the past, a tendency for undergraduate courses in sociology—and in psychology also—to be hangouts for young women not cultivated enough to study literature and not brave or bright enough to study natural science. And I suspect that some of the forbidding terminology and hyperemphasis on methodology in introductory courses in these institutions rests on resentment of this unintended audience, few of whom will pursue graduate study in sociology, and on a stern effort to make clear that neither sociology nor psychology is really about "people" or is intended to help anybody be more human. Page sees women making use of sociology as operators or strategists in civic affairs, for example, in the League of Women Voters. But this too is a use of the discipline not favored by the most highly professionalized teachers. In any event, the sex balance is shifting as sociology grows more muscular and as young men see its relevance—in ways suggested in these essays—for a variety of professional careers. Conversely, the residual resistance to sociology in the "schools of the Ivy tradition"—Page's third type of academic environment—may partly reflect the fact that these institutions are dominated by stag or formerly stag colleges, and that the women's colleges of this category, more hospitable in any case to sociology, have followed their masculine counterparts, perhaps in obedience to the dictum Diana Trilling once expressed concerning Radcliffe, namely, that women must get an education as bad as a man's if they are to believe they are getting a good education.)

The tiresome contempt for sociology in the Ivy schools,

and to some degree among the overpowered people in the humanities along the modern frontier as well, appears to me explicable in part by the near impossibility of a success-ful counterattack against science by the weaker of C. P. Snow's two cultures, for science has prestige as well as power, and in its more theoretical reaches elegance as well as resources, and style as well as earth-shaking and earth-sundering impact. Let me make a perhaps very far-fetched and certainly much too gruesome analogy. Much as the traditional lower-middle classes of pre-Nazi Germany felt unable to attack the great powers of Rhineland industry or Junker agriculture or war-making, and found an available target in the Jews who had the pretensions but not the substance of power, so one can find many humanists whose resentments against the modern world leak out safely in attacks against the social sciences, regarded as holding pretensions to science which they do not deserve and pre-tensions to being socially relevant which they have stolen from the rightful heirs of the humanities.[1]

This gradually eroding disesteem and the corresponding struggle for academic status among sociologists has had divergent consequences in this country and in other coun-tries, as Robert Nisbet (Chapter 3) suggests in his fasci-nating discussion of the consequences of academic organi-zation for sociological creativity. In Germany, where the very eminence of the universities made them the focal point of the struggle of new guilds for recognition, the highly self-conscious effort of sociology to define itself and to distinguish itself from rival social sciences, making clear

---

[1] To be sure, in a reverse twist on this the social sciences are damned as all too social. The fact that they engage in team-work makes them suspect, and the socially uplifting concern they are thought to have, as against a concern for pure or, even better, useless knowledge for its own sake, is another source for derogation. The linkage here reminds one of the nearly vanished linkage of sociology with socialism or social work which may still operate to render its path precarious in centers of fundamentalist or radical right ideology.

that it threatened neither their methods nor their favorite
topics of inquiry, produced not merely a literature of apolo-
getics but the brilliantly clarifying works of such thinkers
as Georg Simmel, Max Weber, and Ernst Troeltsch. In
Great Britain, on the other hand, where down to the end
of the nineteenth century Oxford and Cambridge were
sunk in somnolent complacency, the great intellectual efforts occurred outside of these traditional institutions and
neither thinkers like Herbert Spencer nor observers like
Charles Booth, operating as wide-ranging, unlicensed ama-
teurs, had to worry about academic divisions of labor.[2] In
the United States, in contrast, Nisbet points out that the
struggle for academic status was waged not only vis-à-vis
competing disciplines but in front of a mass audience of
half-educated college students, where one could direct a
share of the traffic towards oneself by appropriate faculty
lobbying and literally toward oneself by writing a textbook
which would be required reading in the absence of ade-

---

[2] Before World War II, Great Britain saw the development of
Mass Observation as a network of more or less amateur social
observers, and more recently the journal *New Society* attempts
to bring the findings and outlook of sociology and other social
sciences both to the layman and the day-to-day practitioner. Mass
Observation did not always stick to what Professor Bressler
might term the Significant, being sometimes pleasantly distracted by the colorful, but I wish both this organization and
*New Society* could be duplicated on the American scene. Perhaps today the British academician both in the old and the new
red brick universities has a sufficiently secure status vis-à-vis
the population at large so as to fear popularization less than his
American counterpart, while British public school traditions of
forensic clarity and elegance survive sufficiently even in a meri-
tocratic Britain so as to fill the Third Programme broadcasts
with literate disquisitions on often esoteric themes. The very
fact that in Great Britain only a small minority attend even the
unestablished universities gives some of those who do both their
amateur outlook and a certain feeling of *noblesse oblige* toward
the enlightenment of the less fortunate. And where the elite
all know each other in person or vicariously, the fear of a
middle-brow invasion from which one takes cover in obscurant-
ism, while not absent, may be somewhat less compelling.

quate libraries (in the earlier days before paperbacks) and in the absence, in the earlier period, of either the resources for research or the leisure for scholarship.

This emphasis on instruction, whether (as in Page's essay) of undergraduates or (as in Marvin Bressler's paper) of prospective school teachers and hence at one remove from all children, or (as in Ely Chinoy's Chapter 5) of American society at large, is increasingly giving way to a more autonomous profession, sustaining itself less by the teaching enterprise and more by its services to specialized clients (business management, medical schools, government agencies, the military, etc.) or to itself. The essays in this volume describe the consequence both for sociological style and for the training of graduate students of these major shifts of audience. Thus while all the writers see sociology as a potentially liberating pursuit for its own sake, a bridge between "the two cultures," [3] and a counterweight to parochialisms of time and space, the essays—and Mr. Nisbet's in particular—argue that the *nouveau riche* status of present-day sociology in America may jeopardize these potentialities. For Nisbet argues that erudition and ripe scholarship are no longer the marks of the teaching sociologist who becomes a doer rather than a cogitator, marshaling squadrons of graduate students for the routinized tasks of his institutes and centers, and rushing them through to put them to work on the assembly line of publication. And Nisbet, Page, and Bressler all observe that graduate students in this process are encouraged both by precept and implicitly to devalue undergraduate teaching, except perhaps for those who can be recruited into the field, and that there are no efforts to train people to become good humanistic teachers in comparison with the efforts made to train them to "do" research. Moreover, they are trained

---

[3] For a companion argument that anthropology and the social sciences generally form a bridge between the two cultures, see "C. P. Snow and the Third Culture" by Lloyd A. Fallers in *Bulletin of the Atomic Scientists,* Vol. 17 (October, 1961), pp. 306-310.

to communicate to colleagues in a shorthand whose actual
redundancy is concealed by apparent ellipsis and graceless-
ness, so that neophyte professionals come to believe (much
more than editors wish were the case) that the style in
which most journal articles are couched is the only accept-
able one if one wants to get published.[4] As an illustration,
Mr. Nisbet quotes a letter from a candid assistant professor:

> I hope I never get tagged in any student election
> or faculty rating as a good man with undergraduates.
> Until my research record is strong and unchallenge-
> able, I am sure I can get farther by mediocre or dull
> teaching of undergraduates because this will at least
> leave open the *possibility* that my research promise
> may therefore be high.

A former colleague of mine who went to teach at one of the
best of the modern frontier universities reported that he
was told by his Department Chairman that, in his teaching
of lower division undergraduates, once he closed the door
of the classroom nobody was interested in what he did for
the next fifty minutes, just so long as he was physically

---

[4] Journal editors themselves sometimes have a compulsion for
compression which is perhaps understandable in the light of the
pressures on them to publish more material than they can
possibly afford to do (cf. on this general problem Derek Price's
chapter, "The Diseases of Science," in *Science Since Babylon,*
New Haven: Yale University Press, 1961), not always realizing
that the bare bones of an article may be more confusing and
take longer to read than a more discursive, aerated, and illustrated treatment. But compression seldom seems to eliminate
the need for repetition in which the authors first give us an
abstract (usually too elliptical to be really helpful), then tell
us what they set out to do (often citing standard works in the
same vein), then what they did do, and finally a pointless
summary which is unnecessary for anyone who has carefully
read the article. The very monotony of these formulae of organization helps deaden many journals. As an occasional reader for
a variety of social science journals, I have often noticed that
fellow readers recommend cutting out case material and other
statistically non-significant but evocative and clarifying detail.

there, and that he should get out again and back to his research with as little fuss or friction as possible. At best, the teaching of undergraduates in many of the most eminent institutions is seen as a weeding-out process, in which only the clearly committed and the exceptionally competent will survive to replace the breed—and in which competence comes to be defined in terms of the model set in graduate school. And this model, Mr. Nisbet contends, comes more and more from the natural sciences and less and less from the humanities where graduate study is seen in part as a prolonged—and often indeed traumatic and destructive—general education which precedes the opportunity to write a dissertation on one's own. Thus it would appear that at the very same time when sociology, although still somewhat marginal in some locales, has won a place for itself in the academic and intellectual scene, it may be losing its relevance as a source of humanistic illumination for the increasing numbers who are going to college and opting for a course or two in sociology—a point brought out in Mr. Page's paper.[5] (To my regret, there is no developed discussion in this book of the possible place of sociology in undergraduate interdisciplinary courses, although Professor Page's discussion of what might be an appropriate undergraduate education for those planning to do graduate

---

[5] There is some discussion of the effort by a number of sociologists to introduce this field into the secondary school curriculum, either under its own name or under a more invigorated version of the social studies. In this writer's opinion, such introduction into the ordinary public school runs the risk of censorship of precisely those anti-ethnocentric and cosmopolitan and critical ideas which, according to the authors of this volume, are sociology's greatest contribution to social understanding. Permitting sociology to be taught by timid teachers under the shadow of no less timid principals and school boards might be even worse than leaving those who don't go to college to encounter sociology in its popular and perhaps slightly less truncated versions in the mass media or in conversation filtered down from the talk of social workers, ministers and rabbis, and other consumers of more or less popular sociology.

work in sociology suggests some of the possible congeries of subjects which might enter into such courses. Furthermore, what is said in these papers concerning sociology might, *pari passu*, be said almost equally well about some versions of cultural anthropology or sociological social psychology, that is, the newer social sciences in general.)

If sociologists pay less and less attention to teaching unprofessional undergraduates, this may mean that the hopes Mr. Bressler expresses for a convergence between sociologists and educationists will stumble—as he himself indicates may occur—over the latter's missionary devotion to the pedagogic enterprise. For Bressler presents a poignant account of the ways in which the educationist (a pejorative term, though not intended by him as such), teaching others, who will in turn teach the great unwashed, feels that he himself must set an example of being accessible to students, and in fact chooses in philosophy and the social sciences those gospels which make a necessity as well as a virtue of such accessibility: group dynamics, cultural relativity, the biological equality of the races, and so on. Thus the teacher and the teacher of teachers tend to eschew the tragic, ironic, oblique, and complex view of life that is fashionable among avant garde intellectuals, including many sociologists. While this may neglect the number of cynics or soured idealists teaching in the public schools, and along with them those Catholics and Fundamentalist Protestants who do not share the general American meliorist view of man, I think that the assessment is in general correct, and that it contributes to our understanding of the defensiveness of educationists, not only vis-à-vis the snobbery of the graduate schools of arts and sciences but vis-à-vis the implicit snobbery of the ideas, the elitist and "new conservative" ideas, often held in those schools. (In the absence of a strong religious or humanist faith, educators find it hard to treat all human beings with fairness and equity without also believing that all people are fundamentally alike and that their apparent differences reflect only cultural disadvantage and not genetic endowment or the kind of Providential testing which Job had to undergo.)

In comparison with professors in schools and departments of education, sociologists are to be numbered among the aristocrats of academia, but the taint of marginality still leads to a certain defensiveness among the latter also, evidenced in the stress in these papers on the ample evidence that sociologists write no worse than other academics and often better. But in general the papers are marked by a good deal of inner security, as in Mr. Chinoy's refusal to be resentful and contemptuous of the chiropractors and osteopaths who parade as sociologists before the general public—he sees them rather (as a few doctors see comparable rival practitioners) as indicating *inter alia* tasks left unperformed by the professional cadre.

As I have said, the task of teaching undergraduates tends increasingly to be neglected or deprecated and is perhaps better performed in practice than in theory. This volume attempts among other things to remedy that neglect, both by directing sociologists' theoretical attention to their own enterprise and toward the educational enterprise in general, and by stressing again what is evident in the great works of emancipation of the last century, namely, how much sociology has to say which can make the average citizen more aware and awake, more interesting and speculative, whether or not it has any direct impact on the quality and texture of our social life.

Professor Nisbet's essay shows how much can be added to our grasp on these matters by a comparative perspective. While I was working on these comments, I was visited by a French academician who had just completed his first tour of American academic and research institutions, and having been here during the summer was startled to discover how rare was the professor who took a long summer vacation for reading, reflection, or even writing, and how common was the practice of summer teaching, attending institutes, conferences, and other round-the-year operations more characteristic of business or medicine. At the same time he was inclined to feel that there was less attention in this country than in his own for the application of sociology to the great future problems of the society as a whole: to the abyss of leisure, the changed character of blue-collar and white-collar work, the effect of the automobile on our cityscapes and landscapes, or the threat of war. Somewhere in the helpful classification of Bressler's paper, where he treats the Actionists, Scientists, and Significance-prone, these matters tend to get lost, for "society as the patient" has no way of institutionalizing its still unawakened possibilities and problems. While applied work is done to meet day-to-day emergencies, the work of the scientist is done within narrow, subdisciplinary tracts, and those who aim for Significance seldom connect even with the sparse data that might at once solidify and qualify their sweeping critiques. Furthermore, comparative work might help us test whether our explanations really explain the extent and location of American introspectiveness, the market both for popular sociology and popular psychoanalysis. Are the Americans so exceptional in this? The Japanese have their own version of curiosity as to how they stand in the eyes of the world, and the Germans for many decades have looked first to England and then to America for tokens of esteem and appreciation, while the Russians today seem notably defensive vis-à-vis the supposedly more cultured (whether in plumbing or painting) Western countries. Yet the Japanese absorb an enormous volume of social criticism from their own purveyors of popular sociology (many of them academicians) without anything like the American interest in psychoanalysis. One wonders to what extent ethnic factors may be relevant here. Indeed the list Mr. Page gives of the products of the New York Municipal Colleges who have now made distinguished contributions to sociology (many of whom would fall in Bierstedt's reference to those who write well) suggests that Jews may have provided an especially osmotic membrane for American as well as ethnic self-consciousness, though this still does not explain the widening market for these wares or the resistance to them on the part of the last-ditch provincials. The diffusion of sociological concepts and ideas, in other words, says a lot about a society and its subdivisions, just as does the diffusion of any set of inventions, some of which turn out to be more exportable than others. Indeed, Bressler's paper discusses the barriers as well as the hopes for the diffusion of sociological ideas in a kind of downward social mobility to a fraternity of educationists who, against the drumfire of such men as Admiral Rickover or organizations like the Council on Basic Education and out of fear of their own weaknesses as well as hope for their own messianic goals, have tended to seal themselves off from those portions of the sociological enterprise which either demand great sophistication in the logic of inquiry or great stoicism in the fact of substantive counsels of despair.

Popular sociology, however, as Chinoy's paper indicates, tries to make the best of both worlds, for on the surface it offers a biting and satirical critique of the reader's own ways of life and those of his neighbors', friends', and mate's; and its implication generally is that things are much worse today than in an earlier, more noble, honest, industrious and yet unrivalrous America. But the latent message is that nothing is expected of the reader, save that he be knowing about all this, possibly even using his knowingness to justify behaving less well than he might be capable of; and nothing is asked of society either, such as radical structural change. Instead, hope is placed, if at all, in a kind of individualistic uplift in which each "organization man" conducts his private rebellion like the good soldier Schweik, only now it is not the soldier but the field-grade officer who sidles away from onerous yet pointless responsibilities. Thus, while Bressler's essay suggests why it is that until recently educationists have looked to psychology rather than to sociology for intellectual nourishment and moral succor, wide upper-middle-brow audiences have put such books as Vance Packard's *The Status-Seekers* at the very top of the non-fiction best seller list. In such fashion, the essays in this book illustrate how sociology can turn back upon itself, examining what it means both for those who consume it and those who fend it off. Unquestionably these changes in both its academic and non-academic constituencies will mean a different recruitment into sociology from that which Page describes for the depression-haunted second generation cadres of the 1930's. We may be permitted to hope that sociology, even when dizzy from success, can continue to attract the academic wayfarer, curious about his place in society and society's place inside him, eager to dispel the parochialisms of his birth in a particular group in a particular moment in history, and eager to make his intellectual living in concern with matters relevant for his own trajectory and that of many others the wide world over.

DAVID RIESMAN

Brattleboro, Vermont
September, 1963

# Contents

\* \*

# Introduction

Since the emergence of sociology in the United States at the turn of the century, the principal preoccupation of most of its practitioners has been—and continues to be, in large measure—the instruction of college students in sociological lore. It was altogether appropriate therefore that President Paul F. Lazarsfeld and his colleagues on the Program Committee, in planning the 1962 meetings of the American Sociological Association, arranged several sessions on the educational functions and implications of the discipline as part of a program devoted to the central theme of "the uses of sociology." The educational component of sociology is a significant matter of course for sociologists themselves, for the growing number of their clients in the classroom and elsewhere, and thus increasingly so for the social and cultural order. Various educational dimensions of the sociological enterprise are clarified by the contributions to this book.

Three of these contributions—Chapter 2 by Robert Bierstedt, Chapter 3 by Robert A. Nisbet, and Chapter 5 by Ely Chinoy—were presented at the 1962 ASA meeting in the session on "The Role of the Sociologist in General Education," and have been somewhat expanded for the present volume. In an earlier version,

Marvin Bressler's Chapter 4 was read at the same meeting in one of the sessions on "The Professions: The Uses of Sociology in Education." Chapter 1 on "Sociology as an Educational Enterprise" was written following the ASA meeting, much of its contents representing elaboration of or response to various points discussed so cogently by my four co-authors. The publication of these five essays under a single cover makes them readily available to sociologists, students, and all readers who are seriously concerned with education.

The five essays treat a single theme: the changing educational role of sociology within and beyond the academy. But each author is concerned with particular aspects of this broad subject. Thus Professor Bierstedt eloquently describes several ways in which sociology, as a liberating and non-provincial subject, and as both a scientific and humanistic discipline, can enlarge "the contours of a liberal education"—when, as I note in the initial chapter, it is taught by educated men. Bierstedt's focus is the intellectual content of sociology. In contrast, Dr. Nisbet, from the lofty and in some respects advantageous position of an academic dean, centers his attention upon the "institutional context" of sociology, the roles of sociologists in colleges and universities, and—in long-term perspective informed by his distinguished historical studies—upon sociology's persistent "struggle for status"; this paper raises several significant problems to be faced if the neglected subject of the sociology of sociology is to be developed.[1] The latter subject, as Professor Bressler's

---

[1] I discuss certain aspects of this neglected subject in Chapter 1 of the present volume; see also the Editor's Foreword to Roscoe C. Hinkle, Jr. and Gisela J. Hinkle, *The Development of Modern Sociology*, Random House, 1954, and Charles H. Page, "Sociology as a Teaching Enterprise," Robert K. Merton, Leonard Broom, and Leonard S. Cottrell, Jr., eds., *Sociology Today*, Basic Books, 1959, Chapter 25.

wise and witty essay brings out, is linked with a sophisticated sociology of education, which until very recently has also received short shrift from sociologists.[2] Bressler discusses similarities and differences between the conventional bodies of wisdom of sociologists and educationists, their contrasting educational roles and environments, and the interplay, present and potential, between them. Among the questions posed by Bressler's paper are those directly related to "mass" or popular education. This phenomenon extends of course far beyond the classroom, especially as it is spread by modern communications including the mounting number of books about social life. More and more of these publications are examples of "popular sociology," the subject of the essay by Professor Chinoy. This development, Chinoy argues, not only reflects the long-standing propensity of Americans for self-examination, but in recent years has been accelerated by both the positive accomplishments and communicative limitations of professional sociologists: popular sociology, whatever its merits or inadequacies in professional terms, becomes a readily accessible part of popular culture.

Sociology as an educational enterprise, then, is a theme shared by these five papers. And they are marked by further similarities. Thus, each essay illustrates the double anchorage of sociology in the humanities and the sciences; and, if I read "between the lines" correctly in my co-authors' contributions, each of us is convinced that sociology should retain *both* characteristics, especially in its educational role. Fi-

---

[2] Strategic problems in the sociology of education ("the next *really* 'hot' field," as Bressler puts it) have been explicated in recent years by Orville G. Brim, Jr., Burton R. Clark, Neal Gross, David Riesman, and others in this country, and by Jean Floud, A. H. Halsey, and Asher Tropp in England.

nally, these papers, although in quite different ways and in differing degrees, are concerned with the shifting images of sociology in various educational and public circles and with educational consequences of these changing conceptions.

CHARLES H. PAGE

*Sociology and Contemporary Education*

# (1)

## *Sociology as an Educational Enterprise*

### CHARLES H. PAGE

The essays following this initial paper raise several matters of sociological and educational concern to which I turn in the present chapter. The rapid expansion and wide diffusion of sociology itself, within the schools and elsewhere, have reached a point that may justify the designation of "Sociology as a Cultural Institution," as suggested in the first division of the chapter. But the growth of sociology, especially in the colleges and universities, has been and continues to be an irregular development, in part at least because of circumstances outlined in the second division, "Varieties in Higher Education," which attempts to indicate some of the social and cultural sources of different intellectual and educational styles in sociology. The concluding division, "The Teaching Enterprise of

Sociology," focuses more specifically upon contrasting educational goals of sociology and upon problems faced by sociologists as educators.

## SOCIOLOGY AS A CULTURAL INSTITUTION

Two of the spectacular, yet generally neglected, changes in this country since the second World War are the incorporation of militarization and of sociology into American life. These developments have taken place on so large a scale and with such far-reaching implications that perhaps they may properly be designated as major social and cultural institutions. I refer to the rise of sociology as "cultural" because it involves, in addition to unprecedented growth and the institutionalization of the field as an academic subject of established substance and theory and as a significant contributor to social technology, an orientation toward social life that is becoming an increasingly widespread ideology. The sociological approach—including the study of social relationships, of group-based patterns of behavior, of functional interconnections among social and cultural phenomena, and a holistic conception of the social order—not only has penetrated the academy in its own name and has infected intellectual life in general (in whatever guise), but has infiltrated the "folk-thought" of our literate, non-folk society. "Ideologically," Talcott Parsons has written, "a 'sociological era' has begun to emerge." [1]

The large increase in the number of "card-carrying" sociologists (membership in the American Sociological

---

[1] The emerging "sociological era," Parsons notes, has followed upon an "economic" era of the late nineteenth and early twentieth centuries and, more recently, a "psychological" era. "Some Problems Confronting Sociology as a Profession," *American Sociological Review,* 24 (August, 1959), pp. 553-544.

Association rose from about 2,700 in 1949 to over 7,200 in 1962) merely hints at the cultural ascendancy of sociology. All universities in the United States—with the laggards Princeton and Johns Hopkins finally succumbing to the trend in 1960—now have departments of sociology (sometimes combined with anthropology) and most of them award graduate degrees in what not so long ago was often viewed as an ill-defined or a disreputable subject; and the large majority of schools permit undergraduates to specialize in sociology, although there remain pockets of resistance at such prestigeful colleges as Swarthmore, Amherst, and Williams. To be sure, there are important regional and other variations among schools (discussed below), but the spread of sociology is impressive: horizontally, from the Ivy-clad centers of educational traditionalism to the mushrooming newcomers across the nation; and vertically, from the freshman year and even earlier to post-doctoral training supported by private and governmental foundations. While most teaching sociologists are associated with liberal arts programs (67 per cent of the American Sociological Association's members in 1950, 59 per cent in 1959), more and more of them are joining the faculties of professional schools— in business administration, engineering, education, medicine, and law, for example.[2] The growing recognition of the desirability of sociological training for future professional practitioners gives promise to the further diffusion of sociology in our increasingly professionalized society.

The assurgency of sociology in the academy is paralleled, though not matched numerically, by the

---

[2] Matilda White Riley, "Membership of the American Sociological Association 1950-1959," *American Sociological Review*, 25 (December, 1960), pp. 915-926; see especially Table 8, p. 921.

march of sociologists into business and industry, federal and local government, and the military services. With economists, psychologists, and other social scientists, sociologists are engaged in tasks involving application of their specialized knowledge and research skills to questions of organizational or public policy.[3] These representatives of "applied sociology" not only help to supply reliable and needed information about social life but some of them are becoming the "social engineers" envisioned by the pioneers Lester F. Ward and Franklin H. Giddings. The United States is not of course approaching Ward's "sociocracy" or Giddings' "societal engineering" (which perhaps is fortunate), but the now-routine employment of sociologists by agencies of great power and influence reflects, again, the firm incorporation of sociology into our national life.

These developments support, but do not confirm, the contention that sociology in this country is becoming a cultural institution. There are more suggestive indications, however, of the cultural impact of sociology than its rise in diverse types of schools and in public and private agencies: these are trends evidenced by the formal roles of official representatives of the field. But sociology, in the view of many individuals (excluding, to be sure, most sociologists themselves), is also "represented" by an expanding assortment of journalists, *personae* of the air waves, and writers of fiction—so much so that Martin Mayer, Steve Allen, and J. D. Salinger, to name a motley threesome, have been publicly proclaimed to be "sociologists." Such misemployment of the term is of course

---

[3] Nahum Z. Medalia and Ward S. Mason have recently reported on the "Position and Prospects of Sociologists in Federal Employment," *American Sociological Review*, 28 (April, 1963), pp. 280-287.

a trivial matter—it has been misapplied for many years to social workers, certain politicians, and socially-minded philanthropists; but the wide adoption by popular writers and public performers of both the rhetoric and general orientation of sociology is a practice of cultural significance. In this respect, sociology joins psychoanalysis and, more recently, a vague kind of existentialism in the market place of middle-brow culture. This popularization of sociology exacerbates problems faced by legitimate members of the guild, a situation discussed by Ely Chinoy in Chapter 5 and one to which I return in the final section of the present chapter.

But the concept *institution* implies more than all of this: the institutionalization of a cultural form involves, in addition to established patterns of behavior, the internalization of a psychological orientation—a set of interests, attitudes, and values—in a substantial segment of the population. That this is taking place in the case of sociology certainly has not been demonstrated empirically, which of course would require a major research effort, but there are, I believe, sufficient surface signs of a likely symptomatic nature to hypothesize a sociologistic trend in the "public" itself. These signs are especially manifest among college students and graduates; they include a growing awareness of the patterning of behavior and belief on the basis of group affiliations, an increasing sensitivity toward and curiosity about the structural dimensions of social life, an interest generally in the "inner-workings" of society (complementing the related interest in the structure and functions of individual personality), and, perhaps, a greater awareness of the important role of painstaking research in obtaining reliable information concerning the social order. These presumed proclivities may help to explain the large consumption of the products of popular sociology, one function of which, it may be argued, is the "confirmation" on the printed page of current folk wisdom.

It may be further argued, although on shakier ground, that what has been called the "American style" is being shaped in some degree by sociology. Parsons, as I have noted above, refers to the present-day emergence of a "sociological era" as an *ideological* development, a formulation that points up cognitive and conscious components of an intellectual stance toward society and social problems. More generally and with much less sense of awareness, the subjective attitudes, objective interests, evaluational tendencies, and, most apparently, the vocabulary of social comment of Americans—especially among individuals who share modal "middle-class" values—are increasingly influenced, I suggest, by a sociological orientation. The plausibility of this speculation may be less convincing than the claim of a somewhat comparable, but no doubt weightier, impact of the cultural institutions of the Negro community, of youth groups, and of sport. Yet each of these "sub-cultures," including that of sociology, clearly reflects the environing social structure and the basic values of the larger society; and each in turn, runs the present argument, affects the inclusive socio-cultural system. Although the mechanisms and consequences of these *interchanges* have received little or no systematic study to date, I shall risk the hypothetical proposition that the institution of sociology, as in the case of the culture patterns of Negro life and youth and sport, is a substantial contributor to the American style.

The social and cultural contributions of emerging institutions are apt to be unnoticed or surrounded by controversy, on the one hand, and, on the other, to induce varied or even opposite effects in different groups and organizations. So in the present case—with respect to both sociology's suspected subtle social functions and its demonstrably significant role in centers of research and learning.

## VARIETIES IN HIGHER EDUCATION

The recent growth of sociology in American colleges and universities has been and continues to be, at once, substantial and uneven. In the academy as a whole, the current prosperity of sociology is evidenced in both quantitative and qualitative terms: by the establishment of independent departments of sociology and social research centers; by the participation of sociologists in interdepartmental and interdisciplinary programs, in which they often play a leading role; by the marked expansion of graduate training in sociology; by the great increase in undergraduate enrollments (which are proportionately larger than the rise in general college enrollments); by the "promotion" of more and more sociologists to deanships and higher academic office; by their achievement of positions of scholarly prestige—sociologists are now elected to the American Philosophical Society and are awarded Guggenheim fellowships without violation of scholarly norms; by their notable activities in such reputable organizations of academic men as the American Association of University Professors; and, as an indication of popular approval, by the appearance of sociologists among those professional elect who grace the television screen. Sociology and sociologists have arrived.

Their accomplishment and status in colleges and universities, however, vary considerably from one type of school to another and among different regions in American society. Comparable institutional and regional variations characterize other scholarly disciplines, of course, but the uneven growth and prestige of sociology stand out sharply, I believe. This variation invites sociological interpretation. In the absence of solid and systematic data, such interpretation must remain speculative (in the manner of much of this essay). Yet casual observation strongly suggests a close association between the development, vitality, and repute of sociology and the nature of its academic— and larger—environment. As in the past, the institutional and cultural *milieux* of sociology today differ substantially in both fruitful intellectual challenge and the often unthinking hard-core opposition from colleagues in nearby and distant fields, in administrative and financial support, and in stimulation from the outside community. Careful study might reveal several patterns of favoring and hampering conditions, but the following comments are restricted to three seemingly distinctive sets of environmental circumstances surrounding the growth of sociology. This growth, though generally spectacular, proceeds at different rates and with different advantages and restrictions in the collegiate habitats of the Ivy tradition, the modern frontier, and the centers of mass education.

## The Ivy Tradition

In major Eastern universities sociology was represented by a few mighty figures during the pioneering decades: by Sumner at Yale beginning in the 1870s, by Giddings at Columbia from the 1890s into the 1920s, and briefly by Ward at Brown from 1906 until his death in 1913. But these men were individualistic scholars and charismatic teachers; they were not the bureaucratic virtuosos needed to organize and develop strong departments manned by sturdy successors. Since their time, sociology has faced, and in some measure continues to face, formal and informal restrictions and has comparatively low prestige in the schools of the *Ivy tradition*, including the "little Ivy" colleges of liberal arts for men and their female counterparts, as well as the universities of the "Ivy League." [4] These colleges and universities are staunch guardians of tradition, generally give strongest support to the humanities and the natural sciences, and display considerable suspicion of the newcomer sociology in contrast with the hospitality afforded the older social sciences.[5] Here, it may be claimed, sociology suffers relative deprivation—in some respects.

In academic communities of the Ivy tradition, however, sociology also enjoys relative prosperity, especially on two counts. The first and quite apparent gain is the conferral of at least fairly high status guaranteed by association with traditionally prestigeful schools: upon sociologists, as upon salesmen in expensive shops, rubs off some of the reputability of the occupational environment. The second, and (if it be so) much more significant, gain pertains to this environment's intellectual stimulation—it presents the

---

[4] The "little Ivy" colleges, Amherst and Williams as noted above, have no sociologists on their faculties (although some educationally subversive teachers in other departments expose their students to sociological ideas and literature); and certain schools in this group, e.g., Vassar, follow the cautious practice of incorporating sociology in such departments of established repute as economics.

[5] Advantages and disadvantages of the older and newer social sciences in the academic context are discussed perceptively by David Riesman in L. D. White, ed., *The State of the Social Sciences*, University of Chicago Press, 1956, pp. 319-339, and in *Constraint and Variety in American Education*, University of Nebraska Press, 1956, Chapter 2. See also Page, "Sociology as a Teaching Enterprise," *op. cit.*, pp. 590-597.

"virtues of adversity." Surrounded by leading lights in other fields, and often regarded from their viewpoint and also by many students as representatives of a suspect subject, sociologists are challenged to legitimize by deed their membership in distinguished scholarly circles. Clearly, not all sociologists rise to this challenge; and, clearly too, schools of the Ivy tradition differ substantially in the degree and kind of intellectual stimulation experienced by the "newer" social scientists. But the outstanding accomplishments of sociologists in several of the private Eastern universities and colleges, I suggest, are in part a product of a pattern of challenge and response.[6]

## The Modern Frontier

These schools include the firmly established California giants and—with accelerating urbanization and industrialization, basic to the development of the "modern frontier"—a growing number of universities in the Northwest, Southwest, and Midwest which also have reached impressive stature in recent years. As in schools of the Ivy tradition, in these newer centers of educational and scholarly prominence sociologists are challenged and respond vigorously with professional accomplishments of a high order. But the challenge is of a different nature and, in some respects, so is the response.

Much of the challenge in these universities comes

---

[6] Continuing with Toynbee's terminology, the severe "adversity" faced by sociology in the Oxbridge environments of England, until very recently, has restricted sociological accomplishments within the academy to London and the "red-brick" universities. But today, though few in number, sociologists at both traditional schools may rise to a "challenge" somewhat similar to that confronted earlier by their American colleagues in universities of the Ivy tradition.

from the outer environment in which they thrive. On the modern frontier, as on the old frontier, traditionalism has a relatively feeble grasp and only mildly restrains the growth of new institutions and deviant cultural ventures, whether "beat" bohemianism, very high divorce rates, the "new radicalism"—or sociology. The modern frontier, moreover, provides the social conditions that in the United States frequently invite sociological inquiry: rapid population increase, heavy in-migration, ethnic diversity, marked physical and social mobility, urban and industrial boom, political and ideological conflict. During the early decades of this century similar conditions stimulated and helped to shape sociology at the University of Chicago, which became for a time the sociological headquarters of this country; today several major centers of sociology are emerging in the widespread area of the new frontier.

If the outer environment of this area presents challenge and stimulation, the inner environment of the frontier universities extends to sociology and sociologists a culturally consistent hospitality. In these schools, newcomers are likely to be welcomed and, once established, their professional performance generally outweighs academic pedigree. Thus sociologists in increasing number have achieved high status, evidenced, for example, by the quality and quantity of their publications, by the kudos of special awards and election to office in learned societies, by numerous invitations from abroad, and, in a mild display of historical irony, by current efforts on the part of universities of the Ivy tradition to entice sociological frontiersmen to move (or to return) to the one-time citadels of American Culture in the East. Understandably, these sociologists are frequently reluctant to leave their present academic homes: faced by encouragement, opportunity, and the stimulation of dynamic surroundings, sociology flourishes on the modern frontier.[7]

Much of the sociology produced in this area's leading universities, I suggest, reflects the dynamic social life, social problems, and cultural ferment of the modern frontier. Thus in recent years its scholars have made numerous and imaginative contributions to several currently salient fields: industrialization, metropolitanization, social stratification, political sociology, militarization, collective behavior, socially rooted problems of the individual life. To be sure, these are fields with which sociologists in schools of the Ivy tradition also are concerned. But their dominant interest appears to be the development of an orderly and highly abstract theoretical apparatus, whether for the study of "macroscopic" or "microscopic" problems, whereas the works of major sociologists of the frontier, though theoretically sophisticated, seem to be closer to the concrete and more directly related to the pressing issues of the day. To overstate the contrast, sociologists in the Ivy centers are apt to be primarily concerned with sociology, sociological frontiersmen with society. These impressionistic comments clearly invite critical reaction. They may, however, indicate (once more) the need for serious study of the social and institutional sources of the sociological enterprise itself.

### Centers of Mass Education

This infelicitous phrase refers to the numerous schools that have mushroomed in all major regions of the United States to meet the ever-growing demand for

---

[7] To be sure, other fields flourish in the "frontier" universities, perhaps most notably the natural sciences. I am suggesting, however, that this hospitable and stimulating environment is especially beneficial for the growth of the behavioral sciences, including sociology.

college education. These include several of the older and a mounting number of recently established state universities, many of the metropolitan and state colleges and junior colleges, and one or two "private" universities on the "subway circuit." These are centers of huge undergraduate enrollments, overcrowded classes and heavy teaching schedules, limited library facilities and standardized textbooks—invidiously referred to as the "educational assembly lines" of American higher education. A large and diverse literature depicts their virtues and limitations; here comment is restricted to the role and status of sociology and sociologists in these schools.

In certain respects, sociology thrives in the centers of mass education, as it does in the frontier universities (some of which also tend to be educational assembly lines). Here, however, the success of sociology is measured less by creative and scholarly accomplishment than by the number of student-clients. Enrollment in the introductory course, especially if the latter is required for a degree, sometimes reaches the thousands, and in such sure-fire subjects as "social problems" and "family and marriage" there are classes of hundreds or more. The sheer massiveness of the sociological educational enterprise guarantees widespread diffusion of at least some knowledge of sociology's perspective and its substance. But huge enrollments usually require the use of predigested textbooks, those scissors-and-paste products known as "readers," "objective" examinations which can be scored by teacher-clerks or by machines, and mass audiences addressed by lecturers who have little opportunity for discourse with their students.

Under these circumstances, the teaching sociologist —particularly the conscientious instructor who tries to "reach" the individual student whatever the obstacles of size and impersonality—rarely can be a productive "teacher-scholar" in the ideal image of the Ivy tradition. If, on the one hand, he treats students in assembly-line terms and, on the other, he is willing to conduct research and to write accordingly, the sociologist in this type of school may be able to build a bibliography at least sufficient for academic promotion. However, unaided by suitable research funds and facilities, in direct contact with relatively few colleagues who offer intellectual challenge, without the help and stimulation of superior graduate students, and lacking those hours of leisure needed for the mind's free play, his publications are likely to lack distinction. In this educational environment, many students are exposed to sociological gospel, sociology may attain an unprecedented (though not necessarily a deserved) popularity, and sometimes sociologists' salaries rival or surpass those of more prestigeful schools.[8] But centers of mass education are not conducive to creative scholarship.

Yet it is in these centers that a principal function of sociology is performed most fully. A creative scholarly opportunity is attached to the role of the sociologist, certainly, but this role also carries an important educational responsibility. The teaching sociologist is a disseminator of social knowledge, a perspective, and a methodology that are, or should be, an increasingly significant part of the intellectual equipment of the educated man and woman—and in these schools he confronts his largest audiences and greatest challenge. Here (as elsewhere) sociology can be dreary recitation of "the obvious" or a spicy segment of popular culture; or, in the hands of an excellent teacher, it can be an exciting and informative exploration of the real-

---

[8] Faculty salaries at the municipal colleges of New York City are among the highest in the country.

ities and possibilities of social life. That this high level
is achieved in many mass educational classrooms indicates the successful accomplishment on a large scale
of a major task of sociology, and in addition is the
source of substantial psychological income for "non-
productive" sociologists. Moreover, effective teaching
demands broad scholarly knowledge and some degree
of creativity: "production" need not—and usually cannot in these schools—take the form of impressive publications.[9]

An historical note is in order concerning the contribution of centers of mass education to sociology itself. Until a decade or so ago especially, certain of
these schools, most notably the municipal colleges in
the New York metropolitan region,[10] provided undergraduate training for many young persons who subsequently made their mark in the natural sciences,
arts, and social sciences. Among these future men of
intellectual distinction was a large number of embryonic sociologists who, as members of faculties of
leading colleges and universities, in recent years have
helped to shape and to enhance the sociological enterprise. Of course, mass educational centers continue
to serve as avenues of upward mobility for aspirants

---

[9] See Florian Znaniecki, *The Social Role of the Man of Knowledge,* Columbia University Press, 1940, for an excellent discussion of scholars or schoolmen and their various types of subroles, especially the distinction between "sage" and creator or
explorer.

[10] On this score (as in other respects), Newark, New Jersey,
must be included. Among the future sociologists who were
undergraduates at one of these schools, The City College of
New York, between the years 1933-1941 and 1952-1953, were
Meyer Barash, Daniel Bell, Morroe Berger, Nathan Glazer,
Joseph Goldsen, Alvin W. Gouldner, Murray Hausknecht, Bernard Kutner, Seymour Martin Lipset, David Matza, Peter H.
Rossi, Stanley Sadofsky, Louis Schneider, Philip Selznick, William Spinrad, Herman D. Stein, and Leonard Weller.

in various fields. But in the 1930s and 1940s the Great Depression, the ascendancy of fascism and the seeming promise of Marxism, political and intellectual ferment, massive social movements, the threat and later the impact of war, the achievement drive of Jewish students strengthened by a high regard for intellectual attainment rooted in religious tradition, and, not least, the availability of inexpensive schooling—all of these circumstances conjoined to create an inner and outer educational environment which stimulated a keen interest in social structure and social change and strongly affected the early biographies of several present-day sociologists of stature. These biographies are an essential source for the study of the sociology of modern American sociology.

Such a study, it must be added, would strongly qualify any depiction of "varieties in higher education" by documenting, in addition to these patterns, the mounting standardization of sociology. Clearly, "homogenization" has not been reached; fortunately, intellectual conflict persists among sociologists, as it does among scholars in all fields of inquiry. In keeping with the norms of scientific growth, however, this happy state of affairs accompanies an expanding area of agreement concerning, at least, the nature of sociology's principal theoretical and methodological problems and, so it seems at times (and as Professor Bressler notes in Chapter 4), a general accepted body of sociological wisdom. This development is reflected in the curricula, the use of "standard" textbooks in both introductory and advanced courses, the choice of research problems by teachers and students (replication of certain investigations has become ritualistic), and, to cite a current fashion, the ubiquity of functional rhetoric in the study of sociology's traditional concerns.[11] These manifestations of standardization are not restricted to this or that type of school: they permeate colleges and universities of the Ivy tradition, those of the modern frontier, and, perhaps with least restraint, the centers of mass education.

A one-time advantage, as well as a handicap, of sociology in centers of higher learning was its conspicuous marginality.[12] Its lack of an assured position in the academy (and in the intellectual world in general) presented sociologists with a large challenge and an opportunity to open up a new frontier of knowledge and perspective. Although marginality and challenge continue to face sociologists today, the former has been lessened by their very accomplishments and by the discipline's resulting gain in prestige, and the latter may be threatened by the complacency of success. But this is hardly as yet a major concern of teachers of sociology.

## THE TEACHING ENTERPRISE
## OF SOCIOLOGY

Sociology as a teaching enterprise is a complex theme. The following comments largely neglect the theoretical and substantive nature of this enterprise and its interrelations with other curricular subjects (which I have dealt with elsewhere[13]); rather they focus upon some of the problems associated with the teaching role itself. An initial—and important—question, however,

---

[11] Cf. Kingsley Davis, "The Myth of Functional Analysis as a Special Method in Sociology and Anthropology," *American Sociological Review*, 24 (December, 1959), pp. 757-782.
[12] I have discussed the marginality of sociology in "Sociology as a Teaching Enterprise," *op. cit.*, pp. 587-590.
[13] *Ibid.*

concerns the aims of sociology as a field of undergraduate study.

## Sociology for What?

At the undergraduate level, sociologists share with
instructors of most other subjects two major and manifest functions: they are participants in and contribu-
tors to general or liberal education, and they are recruiting agents of future members of their own field.
For the great majority of their students, of course,
teaching sociologists perform only the general educational role; recruitment—however rewarding psychologically and however important for the future of sociology—is necessarily restricted to a few enlistees
who view their undergraduate program as preparation
for advanced study and subsequent professional careers. These two educational functions often appear
to be inconsistent or even contradictory, and the paths
to their successful attainment are by no means clearly
marked.

As teachers of a subject studied formally only in
college, and for most students only in the thinly spread
introductory course, sociologists confront both well-
known dangers and less generally acknowledged advantages. There is the danger of superficiality: of treat-
ing complex problems concerning group life in simplistic or one-sided terms, illustrated on a large
(though shrinking[14]) scale by textbooks tailored for
the "student reader" who all too frequently is taken to

---

[14] One indication of the growing academic reputability of sociology, the intellectual self-confidence of teacher-sociologists,
and, not least, the increasing knowledgeability about the "facts
of social life" is the expanding market for theoretically informed
textbooks and other publications of high standard designed for
classroom use. These would have been widely viewed, until
recent years, as "too difficult" for undergraduate students—and,
alas, continue to be so regarded by many teachers.

be, or so it would seem, a participant in elementary rather than higher education. The watering down of complicated and difficult subject matter, including highly abstract theory, constitutes a disservice to the discipline and to the student, of course; moreover, it subverts the goals of liberal education. There is the related danger of attaining popularity at the expense of maintaining high standards, which is clearly a hazard in many fields, but popularity among students seeking mental relaxation and entertainment is an especially easy accomplishment in a subject that necessarily involves the study of both familiar and deviant patterns of social conduct. Here temptation is great—large enrollments pay psychological and, at times, economic dividends—and is abetted by the availability of "easy-to-take" and often titillating products of popular sociology. Finally, there is the danger of teaching the lessons of sociology as if these were all of social science or even the paramount truths of human experience. This propensity may reflect a laudable enthusiasm for one's own field, but it also may take the form of a scholarly provincialism or an outright sociological imperialism;[15] in either case, such a propensity suggests to other members of the academy, teachers and students, that sociologists are intellectually naive, or insensitive to the widespread and cross-disciplinary interest in social and cultural problems, or both. To avoid this impression is not merely a question of teaching tactics: provincialism and imperialism endanger the strategic position of sociology in general education.

Whatever the risks, however, several significant advantages are provided by sociology to its teachers in their general educational role. They are introducing

---

[15] I have commented upon "sociological imperialism" in "Sociology as a Teaching Enterprise," *op. cit.*, pp. 581-585.

students to an increasingly salient mode of inquiry and body of substantive knowledge in our "sociological age." Supported by the long-standing methodological canon of cultural relativity and by the growing emphasis upon comparative studies, they are helping to demote group-rooted and ethnocentric restraints and to promote informed and less biased views more appropriate for citizens of a highly mobile society and a rapidly changing world. In their advocacy of the need for substantiated evidence and rigorous analysis of social data, sociologists, together with other social scientists, aid students to bridge the sciences and humanities: sociology, as Robert Bierstedt stresses in Chapter 2, is linked to both "cultures." And sociologists, if they carry out their instructional tasks effectively, demonstrate that the connection between concrete social reality and abstract social theory is not merely a scholarly preoccupation but rather an essential element of realistic understanding of social life itself. If these represent advantages—and a splendid opportunity—for teaching sociologists, they are also important goals of general education.

Of these several general educational assets, one warrants special comment. Sociologists are often asked, especially by instrumentally oriented students (and sometimes by their parents), about the vocational advantages, if any, of studying sociology at the undergraduate level. Except perhaps as preparation for graduate training in the social sciences (a problematic matter, as indicated below), there is little empirical evidence to support the claim that college courses in sociology are more or less beneficial than those in most other liberal arts subjects as "required background" for specific occupations. But a strong case can be made, I believe, for the contention that undergraduate work in sociology—if pursued in intellectually demanding courses taught by able teachers, it should be stressed—is an especially appropriate educational preparation for a large number and variety of post-collegiate roles. As innovations in professional schools suggest, sociological knowledge and sensitivity are needed more and more in public affairs, law, medicine, social work, journalism, architecture and engineering, teaching, and, with its increasing semi-professionalization, a growing segment of business; moreover, this knowledge and awareness are highly advantageous for women, not only with respect to their roles as wives and mothers—as major strategists of family life, but also with reference to their participation in local and national community affairs—where many female college graduates also occupy strategic positions.

This emphasis upon sociological study as particularly appropriate background for so large an assortment of adult roles may invite the charge of disciplinary near-sightedness or of professional chauvinism. And the following extension of this claim may amplify the risk.

In the dynamic social world of today, successful fulfillment of the roles cited above, whether professional or parental, calls for quick and capable adjustments to rapid and often unforeseen changes. This need highlights the problem of developing educational programs of positive functional service in a swiftly changing and uncertain society. Such programs should alert both potential members of the several "strategic elites" [16] and the general citizenry of our mobile and non-authoritarian society to the inevitability of shifting and new social arrangements, on the one hand, and the stabilizing functions of traditional patterns, on

---

[16] Cf. Suzanne Keller, *Beyond the Ruling Class: Strategic Elites in Modern Society,* Random House, 1963; see especially Chapter 8.

the other. The partial realization (it cannot be more) of this ideal educational goal requires curricular usage of all of the principal humanistic and scientific disciplines, to be sure, although with a greater degree of flexibility and experimentation than currently characterizes the academic scene. But sociology, precisely because it is committed to the study of social structure and social change, can make a unique and significant contribution to general education.

The general educational contribution of teaching sociologists for the most part is made in the same courses in which are enrolled that minority of undergraduates who subsequently become graduate students of sociology (or of other social sciences) with a view to professional careers. The identity and number of these deviants are problematic matters for instructors, who, unless they are saboteurs of their own field, are apt to strive to increase the size and, more importantly, the quality of this aggregate—in competition of course with recruiting agents of other disciplines.[17] In the classroom, then, teachers confront what they may interpret as a divided student audience: a rank and file whose formal schooling in sociology is restricted to college courses, and a handful of neophytes who are destined for graduate training and colleagueship in the sociological fraternity. Yet this division, shakily based upon largely unknown and frequently fickle occupational expectations, constitutes no educationally legitimate ground either for instructional concern or for differential treatment of sociological subject matter at the undergraduate level. Put more positively, *both* general and preparatory educational goals are most adequately served when sociologists (or, say, econo-

---

[17] I have dealt with this type of competition and academic rivalry in "Sociology as a Teaching Enterprise," *op. cit.*, pp. 590-597.

mists, anthropologists, or psychologists) teach the best their discipline affords. A lower standard deprives college students, whatever their future roles, and therefore their society, whatever its future character.

But does not this undifferentiated approach overlook the future welfare of sociology itself? Should not the college curriculum include at least some "preprofessional" courses as, for example, in programs leading toward advanced study in the natural sciences or in medicine? In the case of sociology, undergraduate work in logic, mathematics, and scientific method is advantageous, especially as the theoretical use of mathematical models grows and as "methodology" is increasingly (though incorrectly) identified with quantitative techniques. Sociologists-to-be, however, particularly in view of the fact that most of them, as teachers, will have important responsibilities of a general educational nature, should be encouraged to become men and women of intellectual breadth, which, in curricular terms, calls for study in all three of the conventional divisions: the sciences, humanities, and social sciences. Moreover, in preparing for graduate training, the combination of, say, mathematics–comparative literature–economics or physics–philosophy–political science (plus history in either case) may be more appropriate than a program that includes a large number of courses in sociology. For not only is there apt to be considerable repetition of theoretical, methodological, and substantive materials in undergraduate courses, as well as inevitable overlapping of college-level and graduate offerings, but evidence is lacking of any significant relationship between extended course work in sociology by undergraduates and their accomplishments as graduate students and, later, as scholar-teachers. These considerations support my conviction —which is consistent, I believe, with an apparent implication of Robert Bierstedt's discussion in Chapter 2 —that a "major" in sociology is likely to have less relevance for embryonic sociologists than for other students as a component of liberal education.

## When to Start?

Within the context of formal schooling, the liberal or general educational process begins in the elementary grades, or earlier, and terminates with graduation from college, or later. Training in sociology, a culturally significant part of this process, in fact or potentially, usually is introduced during the freshman or sophomore year, either as one of several alternatives to meet a curricular stipulation in social science or, as in a good many state and metropolitan schools (the mass market for introductory textbooks), as a requirement for a college degree. While these fairly standard patterns, which stimulate large sales and permit market predictability, are welcomed by publishers and, no doubt, by some recipients of royalties, sociologists and other educators hold divergent views concerning the appropriate time for students to undertake the study of sociology. These opinions range from the contention that certain sociological lessons, in whatever classroom guise, should be taught in the secondary or even elementary schools to the argument that exposure to the discipline should await graduate training. Many, perhaps most, sociologists rest content with the academic *status quo,* which generally provides a secure place and promises what appears to be a prosperous future for their subject. But the advocates of earlier and postponed study of the field give voice to alternatives that merit comment.

The number of teaching sociologists who support the view that sociological training should be restricted to graduate schools probably is small. Yet, whether in the give and take of professional shop talk or under more formal circumstances, this view is rather frequently put forth by its exponents, perhaps most of whom are relatively disinterested members of graduate faculties and devotees of scholarly research. Undergirding this view are considerations of educational relevance: sociological study, it is claimed, should be preceded by substantial work in scientific and humanistic fields, a desideratum that strongly suggests the acquisition of the A.B. or its equivalent before entering upon what, at its best, is the demanding discipline of sociology. More specifically, the postponement of sociological training is advocated by some research virtuosos on the ground that understanding of and interest in sophisticated research procedures, mathematical models, and other areas of current methodological concern require a background of appropriate undergraduate study. This emphasis upon curricular prerequisites is closely related to the more general and frequently cited difficulty of coping adequately with problems of abstract analysis which, runs this argument, demands a level of mental maturity and toleration of sustained separation from concrete and "interesting" social realities that is rare among undergraduates: the latters' preference for vivid description of both familiar and exotic features of society rather than "lifeless" abstract theoretical analysis is well known. If, then, the introduction to sociology calls for comprehension of the work of such masters as Max Weber, formal initiation into the discipline should take place when the appeal of such non-sociologists as Vance Packard has weakened or disappeared and when commitment to the field is fairly firm.

The case for the postponement of formal sociological training is based upon what sometimes seems to be a persuasive *rationale*. But this proposal is inconsistent with current curricular trends; and the supporting arguments cited above could be applied as justifiably to economics, psychology, and, increasingly, to political science. Representatives of these fields do not seek to confine study of their disciplines to graduate students—quite the contrary.[18] And, few if any teachers, and not many sociologists, would subscribe to the position voiced over sixty years ago by Edward A. Ross that the realities of "social control" should be revealed only to "clergymen, editors, law makers . . . judges . . . poets, artists, thinkers, and educators": the members of society's "true *elite*" who determine the "ethical" guides for conduct and policy and who therefore should be privy to the actualities of social and psychological life.[19] Today, not only does the search for future members of intellectual and moral elites begin among undergraduate and even high school students, but, in a society committed to democratic values, the development of social understanding among the general citizenry is a commonly accepted goal.

In keeping with this goal and, moreover, as a development that would permit substantial up-grading of college-level courses in the social sciences, certain "sociological" lessons, I contend, should be taught in high school (or earlier). And, ideally, they should be learned by all students, whether members of the college-oriented minority or of the majority whose secondary schooling is terminal. Although most high

---

[18] See e.g., *The Social Studies and the Social Sciences,* sponsored by the American Council of Learned Societies and the National Council for the Social Studies, Harcourt, Brace & World, 1962, especially the Introduction by Bernard Berelson, pp. 3-19.
[19] Edward Alsworth Ross, *Social Control,* Macmillan, 1901, p. 441; for commentary, see Charles H. Page, *Class and American Sociology,* Dial, 1940, pp. 236 ff.

school students (and their teachers—there are exceptions in both categories, of course) are not prepared psychologically or academically to cope with problems of abstract theory and complex methodology, there are several significant matters of sociological relevance that fall within the range of both their capacities and interests. These include basic facts and principles concerning, for example, the socialization process; racial and ethnic differences; cultural variations and similarities (the study of group prejudice and ethnocentrism should be initiated long before the high school years); the universal discrepancy between behavior and ideal norms (high school students are aware of, and often disturbed by, this discrepancy as it is revealed in their own lives and social circles); the nature and ubiquity of social change (the need of "education for an uncertain world" for *all* students is evident today). Some or all of these subjects already form part of "social studies" courses in many secondary schools, but relatively few teachers are adequately trained to provide sociologically informed instruction in either these courses or others in which problems of a sociological nature inevitably arise.[20]

The provision of such training for persons planning to teach in secondary (and elementary) schools is a major concern of many educationists, illustrated by pre-professional curricular changes in Education and by the publication of sociological materials in books

[20] To label high school courses "sociology" (or, say, "economics") may be inappropriate on at least two grounds. At this level, as implied above, instruction in the theoretical basis of the discipline is apt to pay few educational dividends. And, for these students, certain "sociological" lessons may be most effectively taught in connection with such diverse subjects as biology, history, and literature. The lessons themselves, however, should become an important part of secondary—and, in some cases, elementary—education.

designed for courses in this applied and therefore interdisciplinary field.[21] This concern is complemented today by the interest of a seemingly growing number of sociologists in promoting their subject in secondary schools, which is no doubt related to the recent establishment or reactivation of special committees in national and regional sociological associations charged with the task of studying this potential development. Perhaps these organizational efforts reflect in part the imperialistic bent of some sociologists to exploit the vast high school domain (for noble ends, of course), and in part the understandable wish to receive a share of governmental and foundational support already available to other fields for improving their disciplines' contributions to pre-college education. But these expansionist and pork-barrel tendencies probably are far outweighed by the desire of sociologists—and of educationists, as well—to help to construct a school program in keeping with both extant social science knowledge and the needs of students in contemporary society.[22]

## The Sociologist as Scholar-Teacher

Who are the best teachers and what "sociological lessons" should be taught in high school are knotty ques-

---

[21] See, e.g., Blaine E. Mercer and Edwin R. Carr, eds., *Education and the Social Order,* Rinehart, 1957.

[22] For a recent cogent discussion of the introduction of sociological study at the high school level, see Gresham M. Sykes' essay in *The Social Studies and the Social Sciences, op. cit.* After noting various difficulties, some of which are discussed above, Sykes concludes: "Yet I think it is possible and desirable (1) that sociology should be made available as an avenue of study for the academically talented high school student; and (2) that a much more thorough treatment of sociology should be incorporated in existing social studies for all students. Only thus, I think, can we correct a disturbing discontinuity in the study of society" (p. 169).

tions which provoke continuing controversy. At the college level, however, there appears to be considerable consensus concerning the traits of the superior teaching sociologist. Ideally, this paragon has the virtues of an outstanding scholar-teacher in any field: he is, at once, an able specialist within his discipline (and hence eligible for scholarly kudos in keeping with currently predominant standards) *and* a person of broad intellectual cultivation (and hence eligible on this score to carry out the general educational role of undergraduate teaching); he is, at the same time, an enthusiastic and indeed partisan representative of his subject (and thus an inspired recruiting agent for sociology) *and* of sufficiently rigorous standards to discourage those ever-present undergraduates who seek —and usually find—undemanding courses. If these contrasting ideal criteria are generally recognized in the academy, in most fields—including sociology—a Ph.D. degree from a university of distinction also is often cited as a near-prerequisite for effective college teaching: it not only serves to legitimate the instructors' professional status (from the viewpoint of both colleagues and students—the latter are increasingly aware of the "credentials" of faculty members), but, presumably, significantly increases the likelihood of his successful performance of the scholar-teacher role.

Few would question the view that study in a prestigious university is beneficial for the scholarly segment of this bifurcated role. With respect to teaching, however, whether of sociology or of other natural and social sciences, graduate schools have been sharply criticized on two counts: over-specialization and therefore lack of the "breadth" required for effective undergraduate instruction; over-preoccupation with research and therefore disregard of preparation in teaching techniques. Although this double-barreled criticism rests upon unfirm grounds (there is little evidence that specialization precludes intellectual breadth, or that teaching performance is either lessened by research prowess or enhanced by explicit study of classroom skills), it has been voiced for several decades by presidents, deans, educationists, and foundation executives —but not by many "scholar-teachers" themselves. These busy experts in both research and instruction, exemplars of the ideal academic man, are less concerned, I suspect, with shortcomings in graduate training than with meeting the complementary, though sometimes inconsistent, obligations and opportunities of the role of scholar-teacher.

But these comments should not be taken as a quick dismissal of the persistent charge that graduate programs, in ranking universities and elsewhere, are designed to serve the interests of research specialists to the neglect of the needs of future undergraduate teachers. The sources and extent of this criticism have been reported in detail by Bernard Berelson, whose remedial suggestions include supervised (but not merely "menial") teaching experience for graduate students, non-credit seminars "on the character of the liberal arts college and its problems," the development of closer working relations between graduate schools and colleges—with the latter assuming greater responsibility by clarifying their needs and by providing improved conditions for scholarly work—and, on an experimental basis, the introduction of a two-year degree (not the presumably unsalvageable M.A.) tailored especially for college teachers.[23] The latter proposal has been sharply criticized, particularly by those who decry what they view as an inevitably "second-class" degree in comparison with the "true doctorate," but

[23] Bernard Berelson, *Graduate Education in the United States,* McGraw-Hill, 1960, pp. 248-252.

these recommended reforms generally have received considerable attention and frequently enthusiastic endorsement—perhaps an indication of the inadequacy of present graduate training as preparation for the liberal educational teaching task. Neither the universities nor colleges, however, have in any large measure instituted changes along these proposed lines. Realization of the widely acclaimed role of scholar-teacher, when it is achieved, is an individual accomplishment only weakly supported by institutional arrangements.[24]

Whatever the disparity between the aims and methods of graduate training and the tasks of college education, this is of course a situation involving all or at least most of the scholarly disciplines, as Berelson's study makes clear. Yet this is also a situation that confronts the teaching sociologist—and his students—with several problems which derive in large part from both the current fashions and what I believe to be the intrinsic nature of the behavioral sciences. Five of these problems, particularly, present the sociologist in the undergraduate classroom with a special challenge —and, if he is a skillful instructor, with a splendid opportunity to exploit the educational wealth of his field.

First, there is the problem of developing understanding of the *logical rules of analysis* and appreciation of meticulous *methods of investigation*—without swamping students with the nice details of modern research techniques. Clearly, such understanding and appreciation are not matters to be restricted to courses on "methods": questions of analytical procedure, valid

---

[24] The most recent study of the training of sociologists in this country and of related matters, unfortunately not available when this paper was being prepared, is Elbridge Silbey's *The Education of Sociologists in the United States,* New York: Russell Sage Foundation, 1963. See especially Chapters 2, 4, and 11.

evidence, and spurious data are ubiquitous. But instructors recently trained in university "bureaus" or "laboratories," or engaged in their own specialized research, or both, may discount the probability that most of their students do not expect to become social scientists and thus are apt to have limited tolerance of analytical and procedural elegance. Understandably, most undergraduates are more concerned with substance than research technology. The conscientious teacher (unless he holds the view that sociology *is* method) faces the increasingly formidable task of demonstrating how both of these aspects of sociological study are essential and interdependent features of an exciting and significant intellectual enterprise.

Second is the problem of *significance* itself. Research-oriented teachers may give students the impression that sociologists, armed with logical and statistical techniques, are merely manipulating social data in a spirit of gamesmanship, for no other end. More generally, undergraduate instructors have the standing assignment of showing how empirical confirmation of "obvious" folk wisdom is not academic "made work" and is no less important for the growth of social knowledge than the more dramatic sociological discoveries which challenge or refute "what everybody knows." In addition, students, especially if they are encouraged to sample the mounting volume of sociological publications, are exposed to articles and monographs many of which they understandably may view as investigations of trivial aspects of social life or as needless replications; and teachers must (as must authors of textbooks)select and interpret theoretical and research literature so as to discourage its quick dismissal on the ground of "insignificance." To note that certain revolutionary advances in other fields—concerning, say, gravitation or individual psychology—

were initiated by seemingly trivial experimentation or "idle" speculation is insufficient to convince young people interested in the "big questions" about society and human behavior that considerable current sociological work is not socially insignificant. This is a problem with which physicists, to cite the extreme case, need not cope today.

A third problem facing the teaching sociologist is that of revealing the utility, for both understanding and action, of *abstract theory*. Students frequently shrug off the analytical writings of Weber or Simmel or Parsons, for example, not simply because the prose is heavy going, but with the conviction that such highly abstract formulations can have little relevance for the world of the concrete and the practical—here again is the question of "significance." And here, once more, the young instructor, fresh from graduate study and perhaps insufficiently sensitive to the culture of the undergraduate classroom, may be disheartened by the unenthusiastic student reaction to his own theoretical loves. Young and experienced teachers alike, however, if they are ably fulfilling the instructional role, must not only expose the nature of analytical and substantive theory, but must point up the major lesson that realistic comprehension of concrete social life is enhanced, not obscured, by proper use of abstract theory: the folk contra-distinction between the "theoretical" and "real" must be disabused. One helpful procedure in teaching this difficult lesson is to give careful attention to relevant general and special theory in *all* courses. Theoretical issues (as in the case of problems of method) are ever present, and it may be that to "assign" this subject to a typically standardized undergraduate course sometimes discourages the development in students of needed theoretical understanding. In any case, it should be recognized that, while systematic theory is a legitimate—indeed, an essential—sociological specialization, all sociologists in teaching whatever subjects carry the responsibility of bringing out as clearly as possible their theoretical dimensions.

Theoretical sophistication is required for realistic and objective understanding of social and cultural phenomena, and the educational emphasis upon *objectivity* poses a fourth difficulty for the instructor. Of a different order than the three situations outlined above, this oft-discussed problem is shared by teachers of all social and behavioral sciences, although much of the subject matter of sociology and the ameliorative or even radical propensity of many earlier and some present-day sociologists give it a heightened coloring. In the context of liberal education, students, on the one hand, are urged, in their study of social arrangements and human events, to view these in "rounded" terms, to seek "underlying" conditions and "latent" consequences, to distinguish between the essential and secondary or superficial, to remain dispassionate in the analysis of social reality (except of course in the passionate search for scientifically defined truth); on the other hand, they are encouraged, indeed often admonished, to be concerned members of their local, national, and world communities, to avoid presumably socially detrimental apathy, to be "responsible citizens" who will help to build a saner and safer, if not "happier," society. Yet no longer are the goals of reason and progress assumed to be necessarily reinforcing—itself an important historical and social science lesson—and the instructor may be hard put to reconcile "strict objectivity" and social engagement. (The latter, in fact, may be encouraged more easily among less well informed and less analytically minded than among highly knowledgeable young people of scholarly and scientific bent—perhaps a positive social function of relative ignorance.) Many of the teaching sociologist's clients, however, are likely to be enrolled in his courses precisely because of an interest in social problems and their amelioration together with the conviction that social scientists should shun the ivory tower. For such students (and no doubt others), the reminder of the "long-run" social benefits of uninvolved sociological study and of the conventional distinction between scholar and citizen may be construed as inadequate substitutes for, or even as barriers to, corrective social action.

A final problem, known to all sociologists who teach undergraduates and one that can present a severe test of instructional skill, is rooted in what may be termed *folk sociology.* Here, this phrase refers to the considerable amount of reliable social knowledge that all persons must have merely to manage routine roles, but includes as well fragments of information and misinformation, wisdom and foolishness, and firm belief and skepticism about society and human conduct. Folk sociology provides the notorious responsibility of the sociologist of "unteaching," an accomplishment that often must be sought in opposition to such frequently powerful educational agencies as families and friends, informal groups in school and college, and teaching colleagues in various fields other than sociology itself. The strength of folk sociology is sustained in part by a semantic situation, for many of the terms that designate precise sociological concepts are embodied in imprecise folk language—a fact that is apt to try the patience of students and, say, teachers of English, who at times confuse the legitimate use of technical terminology with "needless jargon." Folk sociology also receives support from the seemingly universal propensity of untutored minds to rely upon individual

perspective and anecdote for the interpretation of
social phenomena, and here too the student may have
strong allies among certain instructors in resisting the
non-anecdotal lessons of sociological analysis. And,
with the growing availability of and exposure to the
products of popular sociology, students bring to the
classroom conceptions of this or that aspect of social
life, which refer to important sociological subjects—
for example, social mobility, race relations, delinquency—and may be dressed in the language of sociology; these presentations in the popular media are
rarely free of over-simplification and sometimes are
serious distortions of social reality. Such journalistic
portrayals help to shape the "sociological" views of
college students, who in fact may thus be stimulated to
pursue serious study of the field, but they also frequently complicate the teaching sociologist's unmask-
ing task.

This depiction of the teaching sociologist's varied
assortment of special problems—concerning research
methods, abstract theory, the question of "significance," objectivity and social action, and folk sociology—should not obscure his advantages. These include, particularly, the persistent and widespread
interest in group life and social arrangements (in
"people," as many students say), the growing prestige
of sociology as an academic subject and field of study,
the increase of vocational opportunities for its students, and the recent semi-institutionalization of at
least a sociological rhetoric and perhaps an elementary
sociological perspective: sociology is "in the air."

But these educational assets are less significant, I
believe, than the continuing diffusion among all of the
social and psychological sciences of sociological knowledge—substantive, theoretical, and methodological. If
sociologists laud the innovators of the past and present

who have given sociology its identity and perspective and much of its intellectual attainment, they also should take pride in the fact that economists, political scientists, psychologists, and even a few historians not only employ a "sociological" approach but have made highly important contributions to sociology itself. In this indirect way, as well as in its own name, sociology has already exercised an enormous influence on the study of the changing human scene—and on both counts will continue to do so. If this be the case, sociology as an educational enterprise, under whatever label, has a splendid future.

# (2)

# *Sociology and General Education*

## ✳

## ROBERT BIERSTEDT

Sociology has many uses that are alike unsung and unappreciated. Some of these uses pertain not to its function as an instrument in the acquisition of knowledge but to a rather different kind of function—its function in the course and process of education. I am inclined to think in fact, as I hope the following remarks will show, that sociology is one of the most valuable of all of the disciplines in the university curriculum and that one of its most distinctive virtues lies precisely and centrally in the realm of general education.

Those of us who are engaged in the sociological enterprise ourselves tend to think—perhaps inevitably —that sociology is for sociologists, or at least for those who want to become sociologists. In our colleges and universities, however, we teach sociology to many more than these. It has been estimated that only two per cent of undergraduate students major in sociology and that only three per cent of this statistically small figure go on to do graduate work in sociology. The vast majority, in short, study sociology with no voca-

tional or professional purpose. They appear in our
undergraduate classes and study our introductory
texts either because sociology is required as a supple-
mentary subject in a closely related curriculum or because it satisfies a social science requirement in a curriculum for which another science would do equally
well. There are those in addition, we may suppose and
hope, who study sociology without being required to
do so because it satisfies some wayward or vagrant
curiosity of their own, because it stimulates an intellectual interest, because it has its own intrinsic fascina-
tion. This paper examines some of the educational and
cultural advantages that sociology has to offer these
other groups of students, particularly the last, com-
prised of those who have no intention of making a
career in the field and who have no professional requirement to satisfy. I propose to show, in short, that
sociology has an important role to play in general
education, a role that is wholly commensurate with
and sometimes even superior to the roles played by
such older disciplines as history, literature, and philosophy. I shall maintain that sociology has many virtues that contribute to the cultivation of the intellect
and that it merits a high rank, therefore, among the
liberal arts and sciences.

## THE LIBERATED MIND

The first of the educational virtues of sociology is that,
like all of the liberal arts, it liberates the student from
the provincialisms of time, place, and circumstance.
One of the great disabilities of those who have been
denied the benefits of education is their parochialism,
their attachment to the narrow corner of earth wherein
they dwell. These are the people—and unfortunately
they are the vast majority of mankind—who retain

throughout their lives a primitive loyalty to their initial culture. For the uneducated the initial culture tends to be the permanent culture and only those who travel can learn to minimize the constricting influences of their natal locality. One may say incidentally that this observation applies no less to the urbanite than to the man on a remote ranch or farm. Some of the most provincial of the world's citizens can be found in the largest of the world's cities.

It is not often emphasized that one can travel in time as well as in space. One needs no visas and no passports to visit the Roman Forum in the time of the Caesars, to watch the coronation of Charlemagne on Christmas Day in the year A.D. 800, to participate with astonishment and shock in the excommunication of Spinoza, or to study with Darwin the giant orchid of Madagascar. This, of course, is one of the advantages that history confers upon those who would read its pages and thereby invite seduction by Clio, the most attractive of the Muses.

One may ask, however, why history should be superior in any way to sociology in exercising this liberating function. History can free the receptive mind from the limitations of time and space by removing it to other times and places, to other periods and climes. But sociology can do more than this. Sociology can liberate the mind from time and space themselves and remove it to a new and transcendental realm where it no longer depends upon these Aristotelian categories. For the historian, liberated from his own time, is apt to become engrossed with another, and to become again a captive of a particular time and place and circumstance. The sociologist, on the contrary, transcends all times, all places, and all circumstances in his effort to find the universal principles that characterize human societies everywhere, whether they be large or small, ancient or modern, Eastern or Western, primitive or civilized. This sociological liberation, of course, is liberation from the concrete, as all scientific liberation must be, and in this sense any movement from the concrete character of history to the abstract character of sociology brings a sense of freedom and of intellectual expansiveness. It is a freedom which responsibly enjoyed and maturely exercised, gives stature to intellect and thus serves one of the ends of education.

This sort of liberation, in a world beset by provincialisms, by the ethnocentrisms of culture and the temporocentrisms of era, period, and century, is no mean or insignificant accomplishment. Whether the group that claims our parochial loyalty be race or region, or class or religion, or neighborhood or nation, we are all influenced by it and, when uneducated, controlled by it. Sociology helps us to free ourselves from these particularistic controls and to learn to see a more universal society and a single human race. To see the eternal in the passing present, the universal in the particular fact, and the abstract in the concrete event—these are among the gifts of a liberal education. They are also the mark of the free man which it is the function of a liberal education to create.

It is good for the undergraduate, in short, to realize that there are other races and regions, classes and religions, neighborhoods and nations, and it is even better to recognize that beneath the cultural differences and diversities that appear upon the surface all human societies are in essence the same. They have the same basic structure and form and shape, they arise from similar causes, and pursue in many cases a similar destiny. And it is sociology, which concentrates upon structure and form and shape, that contributes this sense of similarity and of universality to the educational process. One may say, therefore, that whatever it may teach us as a science, sociology also belongs to the liberal arts, and like history, philosophy, and literature, has a liberating influence upon those who are fortunate enough to be exposed to its teachings, to its probes and its quests, its contexts and its styles.

## THE ABSTRACTION OF INQUIRY

The second of the educational advantages of sociology —a corollary of the first—is that it introduces the student to the nature and function of logic and scientific method. The introductory course in sociology teaches the student, for perhaps the first time, something about the processes of abstraction, of rising by induction from concrete fact to abstract principle, from datum to generalization, and from observation to understanding. The student learns to deal not only with the concrete and the tangible but also with the abstract and the intangible. Events, persons, and situations are all concrete and factual, easily perceived or easily recalled, and often well remembered. They exist as objects of knowledge on the level of immediacy and of immediate confrontation, needing no guarantee of meaning or of validity in order to occupy the mind. How different in this respect are the intangibles of sociology—culture, norm, folkway, law, sanction, status, role, institution, power, authority—none of which is susceptible to the immediacy of sense experience. Indeed, it may be in sociology that the student learns the logical functions of class inclusion, class membership, and class identification, and subjects to logical manipulation and inference concepts that are already several steps removed from the phenomenal world in which he has been accustomed to move and in which he makes his common observations. It is in this way too that he learns the nature and character of definition, and the rules of measurement. It may be that in these respects the role of sociology is almost unique. For in the humanities the scientific method plays no part and in the sciences it is taken for granted. It is especially in sociology that it rises to the level of awareness and becomes a matter of conscious application and employment.

## THE SENSE OF ORDER

A third educational consequence of some importance, one also related to logic, is the sense of system and of order that sociology exhibits, and which is a normal and even inevitable accompaniment of the introductory course. I do not mean by this the theory and practice of artificial systems, of systems of nominal definitions, systems of descriptive equations, mechanical systems in equilibrium, biological systems in homeostasis, or logical systems whether open or closed. I mean instead something more substantive and empirical—namely, the sense of order as order applies to a specific body of knowledge and in this case to a body of knowledge about society. A science of sociology is possible only because society itself is neither chaotic nor anomic but exhibits instead recurrences and regularities, patterns and configurations, and these are evidence of the existence of order. Anyone who examines human events in a search for patterns is *ipso facto* a practitioner of the science of sociology. The student who is encouraged to do this regularly learns to look behind appearances and to see the structure that constitutes an order. He confronts in this way the problem of induction in its practical application to an intellectual exercise. He has been acquainted with deduction, as it were, ever

since he met in plane geometry the axioms of Euclid
and learned to parrot the propositions that lead, for
example, to the proof of the Pythagorean theorem.
Now he learns—and introductory sociology has this
to teach him—that there is another logic as well, the
logic of induction. For it is in sociology that the
idiosyncrasies of custom disappear in the logical
process that gives category and classification to them
and finds form and structure in the societies that con-
tain them.

Philosophers may not yet be able to explain what
induction is—they may in fact make all of the Baconian
errors in their effort to use it and they may even deny,
with Bertrand Russell, that it is anything more than
an "educated guess." But the need for induction, if
properly articulated, attains an unusual clarity in sociology. The student is thus doubly blessed—once with
the sense of order, which it is the function of knowledge to impose upon the universe, and once again with
the logical process involved in achieving it. I hasten
to confess, of course, that few students of introductory
sociology are aware that these wonderful—and won-
derfully logical—things are happening to them. But
they are there nevertheless, in the nature of the sociological enterprise, and cannot help but make an impression, however dimly perceived.

These things contribute indeed a methodological
sophistication that it is not possible to parallel in the
case of some of the other disciplines. In the sciences,
pedagogical activity is often dissipated into the repetition of purposeless experiments as remote from genuinely scientific implication as they are from human
concern. In the humanities, the second of C. P. Snow's
two cultures, scholarship often disintegrates, in its day-
to-day academic setting, into the dry rot of textual
exegesis and sectarian criticism. Indeed, the ill-natured

attack of F. R. Leavis upon Sir Charles is an indication of what can happen when the humanities themselves cease to be humanistic and liberal and become instead something hypercritical, carping, and querulous.

Sociologists, in contrast, have been forced by the sheer intrinsic difficulty of their enterprise to acquire a kind of methodological sophistication that is lacking in these other endeavors. As suggested above, the humanists need no philosophy of science; they know little logic and less metaphysics. The scientists, on the other hand, are so accustomed to their methods that most of them have long since ceased to inquire into their logical or epistemological foundations. Both groups, in short, are innocent of methodology, which is the logic of inquiry. They are innocent, that is, of philosophy. As for the philosophers themselves, they, of course, have ceased to exist—except at Oxford University where they indulge themselves in a sterile kind of enterprise called "analysis," an enterprise that depends wholly upon Oxford cloisters and no longer has any connection with a world in which order is observed and knowledge acquired. It is in the social sciences, in our century at least, and especially in sociology, where men confront major methodological issues and it is sociologists in consequence who acquire the kind of philosophical sophistication that no longer accompanies these other inquiries.

It is sometimes asked why those who have made the most important contributions to the sciences—men like Newton and Darwin and Einstein—have expressed the fewest sentiments and opinions on the philosophy of science and, on the contrary, those who were not notable for their scientific achievements have frequently made pronouncements of repute about the nature of science. Francis Bacon, for example, for all of his practical empiricism, his pragmatic induction, and his

disdain for "received opinion," made no contribution
to any of the sciences and was the last of the great
European intellectuals to refuse to accept the helio-
centric hypothesis of Copernicus. It may be that
those who are close enough to science to practice it
without methodological question or constraint are too
close to observe it with methodological criticism and
concentration. On this score, sociology occupies a
middle position, as it were, close enough to use but not
too close to abuse, or to use uncritically. This position,
of course, may be an impediment in the acquisition of
knowledge, but it is an advantage in enlarging the
contours of a liberal education.

There is still another factor involved in the methodological sophistication of sociologists. Physics, astron-
omy, and the other natural sciences made some of their
greatest strides before Immanuel Kant asked his embarrassing and difficult questions about the possibility
of constructing synthetic judgments *a priori*. I do not
mean to imply that the problem of knowledge has its
origin in *The Critique of Pure Reason* but I do mean
to say that post-Kantian thinkers, a category that includes all sociologists, have had to contend with Kant-
ian questions whereas pre-Kantian thinkers did not.
The point is that if methodological sophistication is a
virtue then sociologists, because of their post-Kantian
place in intellectual history, have a larger opportunity
to acquire this virtue than the protagonists of the
earlier and more settled sciences. Stated another way,
sociologists can make an educational opportunity of an
historical necessity.

### THE TWO CULTURES

We have still other advantages to emphasize on behalf

of sociology. There are bridges after all between Snow's two cultures and one of the strongest of them, one of the most convenient and most serviceable, is the science of sociology. In the British educational system, where specialization is an early requirement—often beginning as early as the sixth form, which is below the university level—it is easy to understand why those who know the sonnets of Shakespeare are not similarly conversant with Avogadro's Law. Between letters on the one hand and science, especially experimental science, on the other there runs a river that is difficult to cross. Those who live and work on one bank of this stream have few acquaintances on the other and their relative isolation, their social distance so to speak, results at long last in separate languages and finally, for that reason, in two cultures. In the United States this situation is leavened in some measure at least by the absence of early specialization and by the encouragement of graduate work in fields quite distant from one's undergraduate concentration.

But it is leavened even more, I believe, by a strong social science tradition and especially by the development of sociology in this country, a development which has been nowhere near so rapid in the United Kingdom. It has been noted frequently that sociology shares its subject matter with the humanities and its method with the sciences, and in this sense it clearly participates in both of the two cultures. This point can profit by renewed emphasis, and particularly perhaps by the reminder that bridges have an equal purchase on both banks of whatever stream they span. Sociology is a science in premise, approach, and method, but nothing human is alien to it, and it belongs therefore almost uniquely to both the sciences and the humanities.

## PERSON AND SOCIETY

Still another virtue of sociology is that it stimulates
reflection on the oldest problem known to social philosophy, that is, the relationship between the individual
and society. The problem, of course, is ultimately a
philosophical one, and not properly sociological at all,
but of all the disciplines in the curriculum sociology
provides the widest and the best-paved avenue of approach to it. For it is in sociology that the student is
most likely to discover the ways in which the structure
of his society, the content of its culture, and the
character of its norms all help to socialize him, carv-
ing out of the biological material the person that he
has become. What then is the relationship between this
person and his society? What does each owe to the
other? Where in "the vast intrinsic traffic of society,"
where in the welter of social process, where in the
eternal changing juxtapositions of groups does the
individual discover his own identity? What guarantees
his integrity as an individual and confers upon him
the irrepressible and unrepeatable character of his own
personality? These questions, as I have said, belong to
social philosophy, and to them men in each succeeding
historical era may have a different answer. But sociology supplies the base, the point of departure, from
which intelligent and thoughtful answers can proceed.
We shall always want to know the ultimate meaning
of Aristotle's assertion that man is a social animal, and
it is in the study of sociology that the student can
gain his first appreciation of its profound significance.
This too is one of the educational rewards of a course
in sociology.

## SOCIOLOGY AND HISTORY

We would say, as a penultimate point, that sociology belongs not only to science and to philosophy but also to the sweep of history. For there is a place, and an important place, for sociology in the history of human thought. Whether we begin with Plato in one tradition or with Confucius in another, the nature of human groups, the character of human relationships, and the profiles of human societies themselves have always attracted the restless and inquisitive mind and have stimulated it to reflection, to speculation, and finally, in the nineteenth century and in our own, to scientific inquiry. It is a history that reminds us how short the distance we have travelled, how long the road ahead. But it is a history nevertheless that has its peaks of scenic beauty and of scientific truth, of radiance and significance.

It is with respect to history too that sociology asks its most penetrating questions. For sociology is not content with description, however thorough it may be, or with analysis, however profound. It has a more fundamental quest. It seeks also the causes of things—things as they are and as they have come to be. Behind all of our research and all of our theory there lies the desire, often subliminal, to find a meaning in the ebb and flow of human affairs, in the systole and diastole of human history. This may well be the most profound and the most difficult of all questions. But there is no doubt that it is a sociological question, the question in fact that motivated Auguste Comte to found our science and to give it a name. For when the philosophy of history leaves its theological and metaphysical stages and enters its positive stage it becomes identical with the science of sociology. As this, the most important of the Comtean insights, continues to inform our discipline so also will it stimulate our students too to discover this area of intellectual inquiry. Nothing more important than this could happen to them in the entire course of their liberal education.

## THE PROSE OF SOCIOLOGY

I turn finally to a sociological virtue of an entirely different kind. It may seem surprising to say so in view of the frequent—and frequently ignorant—attacks upon sociology in the public press, but in sociology as in other fields there are literary craftsmen, people who use the language with grace and skill and style, writers whom it is a pleasure and even a delight to read. Our critics have so often crucified us for our jargon that we have come to believe the criticisms ourselves. Entirely unnoticed in this process is the literary quality that illuminates some of our books and papers and that confers distinction upon our prose endeavors. We do of course—it would be idle to deny it—have our offenders against that noble thing, the English sentence, people who have forgotten, in E. M. Forster's words, that "When prose decays, thought decays, and all the finer lines of communication are broken." It has been too easy to berate sociology for the stylistic infelicities of some of its practitioners, and several journalists, with no recognizable style themselves, have had a try at it. It is time to say to these critics that sociology too has its stylists and that the best prose in sociology can stand comparison with the best in any field.

This view is so far removed from common and public observations that a few examples may not be amiss. The first of these might well be the late Florian Znan-

iecki, whose English prose, like that of his country-
man Joseph Conrad before him, has the power to
elevate the mind and to stir the intellect into recog-
nitions and reminiscences of aesthetic significance.
Among Znaniecki's books I should like to mention particularly *The Social Role of the Man of Knowledge*,
based upon the lectures he delivered at Columbia
University in 1939.[1] This little book is a literary gem
—a work distinguished by a style that is rare in any
language. My second example is Gabriel Tarde. Few
who read the following passage, which Tarde wrote
about sociology itself and the sense of order it seeks to
delineate, can fail to give it a place among the splendid
paragraphs in the world's literature:

> When we traverse the gallery of history, and ob-
> serve its motley succession of fantastic paintings—
> when we examine in a cursory way the successive
> races of mankind, all different and constantly chang-
> ing, our first impression is apt to be that the phe-
> nomena of social life are incapable of any general
> expression or scientific law, and that the attempt
> to found a system of sociology is wholly chimerical.
> But the first herdsmen who scanned the starry
> heavens, and the first tillers of the soil who essayed
> to discover the secrets of plant life, must have been
> impressed in much the same way by the sparkling
> disorder of the firmament, with its manifold meteors,
> as well as by the exuberant diversity of vegetable
> and animal forms. The idea of explaining sky or forest
> by a small number of logically concatenated notions,
> under the name of astronomy or biology, had it oc-
> curred to them, would have appeared in their eyes
> the height of extravagance. And there is no less
> complexity—no less real irregularity and apparent
> caprice—in the world of meteors and in the interior

[1] Florian Znaniecki, *The Social Role of the Man of Knowledge*,
Columbia University Press, 1940.

of the virgin forest, than in the recesses of human history.[2]

These two examples, of Znaniecki and Tarde, do not imply that the stylists in sociology have all departed, along with Small and Ross and Cooley and Tönnies, and that those who remain are butchers of words and despoilers of sentences. On the contrary, it is quite easy to compile a list of contemporaries who respect the English sentence and whose writing merits applause not only on sociological but also on aesthetic grounds. A little reflection inclines me to believe that our poor writers are in the minority and that our critics take extraordinary pains to find the jargon of which they then complain. I should maintain in any event that the literary quality of many of our works is an additional boon to the student of sociology.

In the course of this paper I have mentioned at least seven of the contributions that sociology can make to a general and liberal education. In the first place, like history in particular, the study of sociology liberates the student from the provincialisms of time, place, and circumstance and frees him from the constrictions of his natal culture. Secondly, it introduces him to the role of logic and of scientific method in the acquisition of knowledge and thus contributes, thirdly, to his sense of order and to his methodological sophistication. In the fourth place, sociology is a discipline that spans two cultures, the scientific and the humanistic, using as it does the method of science to explore the concerns and affairs of humanity. In the next instance, the fifth, I suggested that sociology initiates and keeps at the front of student awareness the ancient problem of the relationship between so-

---

[2] From lectures delivered at the *Collège libre des sciences sociales*, 1897. Reprinted in Robert Bierstedt, ed., *The Making of Society: An Outline of Sociology*, Random House, 1959.

ciety and the individual. As a sixth point I referred to another ancient problem, the meaning of history, and declared that the philosophy of history, when it becomes positivistic, is indistinguishable from sociology and that it is the responsibility of sociology ultimately to find an answer to this age-long quest. Finally, in opposition to those who accuse sociologists of stylistic inadequacies, I maintained that the literary quality of their work is not one whit inferior to that which can be found in other learned disciplines.

These things are good for the student to learn and to experience. They are part of a general education. They are among the virtues that sociology has in store for those who, not necessarily wanting to become sociologists, nevertheless seek in sociology some acquaintance with a great and liberal tradition. These virtues are available also, of course, to those who pursue professional careers in sociology, but these comments concern primarily the others, who are in the large majority. For them especially sociology can be like those crops that George Berkeley mentioned in his *Commonplace Book*: "crops that are planted not for the harvest but to be plowed in as a dressing for the land."

# (3)

# *Sociology in the Academy*

## *

# ROBERT A. NISBET

I will be concerned with sociology in this paper solely as an academic discipline and with sociologists only in their academic roles. Any discussion of the intellectual content of sociology, its problems, themes, and propositions will be largely incidental to this special interest. It is the institutional context rather than the intellectual substance that is central, although, as I shall indicate, the two are by no means unrelated.

It must be emphasized that sociology, even more than its sister disciplines, economics, political science, history, and psychology, has been from the very beginning in this country an overwhelmingly academic enterprise. Until a couple of decades ago it was an exceptional sociologist indeed who carried on his work outside academic walls. One need only compare the memberships of the several professional societies in the social sciences to get a notion of how pre-eminently academic sociology was during the first half century of its existence in the United States. The other social sciences, including history, always had, even in earliest years, a substantial number of non-academic members. This was much less true, however, of sociology. So far as I am aware, no president of the American Sociological Association[1] has ever been elected who was not from a university or college whereas in other social science professional societies it was not uncommon, in earlier days at least, for individuals to be elected to presidencies who had no academic affiliation whatsoever. More to the present point is the fact that until fairly recently research objectives, orientations, and skills were shaped largely by the academic world in which they existed. Omitting (as we must) social welfare, we are justified in concluding that it was a rare sociologist indeed who operated in ways other than those prescribed by academic norms.

All of this has changed substantially, however, during the past twenty years and especially during the past ten. Sociologists are to be found today in rising numbers in government, the professions, industry, and other areas. The emerging character of sociology as a profession distinct from the university has inevitably affected the discipline, including the roles of sociologists, and what I shall be concerned with primarily in this paper are some of the consequences of this development. Alterations of role, conflicts of self-image, and feelings of marginality are becoming as noticeable in sociology as they are in other social and cultural systems subjected to sudden change.

There are four tendencies that are particularly important. All of them, it must be noted, are equally manifest today in other disciplines in the social sciences and, even more noticeably, in the natural sciences. It is the relative suddenness and recency of their

---

[1] The American Sociological Society was established in 1905, retaining that title until 1959, when the name was changed to "Association."

impact in sociology that gives them extraordinary significance at the present time.

## THE BLURRING OF THE ACADEMIC IMAGE

It is becoming increasingly difficult to distinguish the professor of sociology from the non-academic professional and even from the administrator. It used to be said that there was more difference between two professors one of whom was an administrator than between two administrators one of whom was a professor. This may still be true in certain areas of the university curriculum, especially in the humanities, but for the physical or social scientist engaged more and more typically in large scale research, working on an around-the-calendar basis, housed in special institute or laboratory quarters, equipped with staffs of secretaries and technicians, with budgets to prepare, with payroll sheets to fill out, it is difficult for the individuals involved not to look and feel more like civil servants and business men than like faculty members traditionally conceived. Add to this the sociologist's rising number of governmental, professional, or industrial consultantships, his memberships on governmental and other advisory committees, and his almost ceaseless travel to meetings and conferences, and the traditional image of the academic man seems less relevant than does that of an executive or bureau chief.

It is very easy, given this kind of existence, for such traditional matters in the university as curriculum, academic policy, student advising, and even teaching itself to seem dull and unworthy of the talents of a distinguished mind. Universities—good ones at least—have always depended upon a vast amount of unofficial administration from their faculties in the form of unpaid department chairmanships, policy committee memberships, and related activities. The faculty's proper concern for its intellectual freedom was matched by an equal concern for participation in the governing of at least the curricular areas of the university. At the present time, however, it is becoming more and more difficult to enlist the full interests of the distinguished members of the faculty in these vital areas. They are, after all, time-consuming, as well as unpaid, and it is not easy for them to compete successfully with the opportunities for professional advancement that lie outside the university and carry both remuneration and honor.

No doubt I exaggerate somewhat the diminishing character of the sociologist as first and foremost an academic man. But, allowing for some exaggeration, it remains true, I believe, that the traditional image of the professor as someone who is primarily a teacher, a molder of character, a gentleman tinged slightly with unworldliness, a man who thinks otherwise and who tends to recoil at the thought of administration and its demands, hardly fits the realities of academic life in many departments of sociology today. The difference between academic and non-academic used to seem very sharp. Today, frankly, it does not. Whether this blurring of academic identity, this blurring of the line between the academic and the administrative-professional is good or bad is, of course, impossible to foretell.

### THE DECLINE OF SCHOLARSHIP

This phrase need not be interpreted lugubriously. Scholarship is not the timeless equivalent of research and thought, a *summum bonum*. It is, like epic poetry or the novel, a form of intellectual expression and, like any form, distinguishable from its content. Scholarship has certainly not disappeared from the sociological scene, but it is increasingly rivaled by forms of expression which, making no claim to scholarship in the traditional sense, must be seen as research reports and memoranda, and this seems to me to be true whether these reports are of book length or article length.

The typical research contribution of the academic man a generation or two ago was the book, the essay, or the formal lecture. Almost universally these were written by the man alone, rarely in single collaboration and virtually never with a group or team. A certain elegance was expected—and found in the writings of such major figures as Sumner, Cooley, Ross, Small, and Giddings—that extended itself not only to the style of writing but to literary and biographical allusions, to footnotes and references, and in the continuous efforts to draw from as large a context of knowledge as possible.

The format of scholarship tended to put a premium upon wisdom and experience as well as brilliance or command of data, and the net effect was to emphasize the likenesses between the social sciences and the humanities in their characteristic expressions. Scholarship tended to have a middle-aged and even leisured quality about it, the results of a system in which younger academic persons rarely did research —their job was teaching; research would come later as a privilege—and it was carried out almost wholly in long summers, free from curricular or other distractions and free also of the implicit threat of publish-or-perish.

I repeat, scholarship does indeed continue; there are mavericks who cannot endure the discipline of the institute or research team. But there is much reason, I am inclined to think, for believing that the typical product of research today is more likely to be a report with multiple authorship running as high as eight or ten, making the title page look sometimes like an advertising agency or law office letterhead. The enormous emphasis placed by faculty promotion committees and deans on research productivity, even for the assistant professorship, the professional competitiveness and the sense of getting there first in publication (previously known chiefly in the physical sciences) combine to make almost impossible today that steeping of ideas and results that scholarship in the older sense demanded and that the institutional context once made possible. The drive for professional eminence is departmental as well as individual today, and because of the heavy premium that departments perforce place upon rapid rates of publication for their members, it is less likely, I think, that the scholar will be sought by dynamic departments than will the individual who can work comfortably and creatively within projects and specialized centers.

Here also, then, the difference seems to narrow between the academic person and the non-academic researcher. The work done today by research teams and organizations outside universities is frequently difficult to distinguish in type and format from the research coming out of universities. This being the case, the difference between the academic and the non-academic researcher may come to seem irrelevant, as it so largely has in the natural sciences.

Has the change in format of research taken its toll in style and manner of writing? Undoubtedly it has. Style, like form, tends to follow function. Because of the widening tendency toward the research report, in contrast to the work of scholarship, a certain selective survival value comes to be attached to writing that is as free as ingenuity can contrive from the literary graces. Learned allusion, paradox, simile or metaphor, wit, and emanations of personal wisdom are expendable. The data are the thing, coupled with lean, terse inferences. At best this can make for spare and masculine prose; at worst, however, it can read like a bill of lading.

The only really lamentable part of the whole process seems to me to be in those rare cases where individuals have considerable literary aptitude—and who could write superbly if they would, as Fermi, Gilbert Lewis, and Oppenheimer among physical scientists have written—but who choose instead to hide these aptitudes on the ground that if their writing shows undue grace it may be interpreted as irrefutable evidence of an unscientific mind. Too many of the younger and able members of our profession tend to think of style as flabby ornamentation when it should be thought of as muscle.

## CHANGING CRITERIA OF ACHIEVEMENT

It is today extremely difficult for a sociologist—or any other scientist or scholar—to win prestige in an academic environment on the basis of the largely moral or "human" qualities that in decades past gave certain faculty members marked influence on the campus even when their scholarly and professional fame was slight. Related to this is the decline in eminence on the campus of the broadly cultivated mind as compared to the specialist or expert. One remembers that Max Weber, in his treatment of a typology of educational systems, pointed to two opposite types of teachers: the one, he said, was designed to "awaken charisma"; the other "to impart specialized expert training." It is reasonably clear, I believe, that the second has become largely dominant, though I would not wish to suggest that the two types are irrevocably separated: there are of course a few rare charismatic specialists in our midst.

This change in the criteria of prestige and achievement can make for minor tragedies in academic life today, especially in the small liberal arts college that has traditionally emphasized qualities in a faculty member that might be expected to "awaken charisma." Consider the plight of the sociologist in a certain celebrated small college that I have been told of. Campus tradition requires that the faculty member's office door be open to students all hours of the day, except when he is at class, and students, I am told, are relentless at this college in their insistence upon the open door policy. But with inconsistency verging on downright betrayal, the same students will often ridicule their professors because they lack the research reputations held by faculty members at a neighboring university.

There is a rising tendency even on the part of undergraduates, including a few precocious freshmen, to rate their teachers less in terms of qualities that traditionally have counted and that undergraduates might be presumed to be competent to judge—"interesting lecturer," "devoted to students," "real human"—and more and more on what filters down to them about the professor's general research eminence and his national professional reputation. Is the day too far off when one may overhear an undergraduate saying "Take Jones' course; he just got a half million from NIH" instead of the more traditional type of undergraduate recommendation?

The familiar characterization of a faculty member being a good teacher but a poor research man (which is apt to be fatal today in an academic institution of quality) has led to many a naturally good teacher deliberately hiding this particular light under a bushel lest he thereby be thought necessarily without promise as a research man. As one candid and cunning assistant professor put the matter to me in a letter: "I hope I never get tagged in any student election or faculty rating as a good man with undergraduates. Until my research record is strong and unchallengeable, I am sure I can get farther by mediocre or dull teaching of undergraduates because this will at least leave open the *possibility* that my research promise may therefore be high." Here too students, especially graduate students, have absorbed the shift in values, and one detects a certain suspicion among the more sophisticated students of the faculty member whose teaching scintillates.

Much of the basis of the change I am here concerned with lies in the modified character of research in the social sciences today. There are two kinds of research: the kind that is compatible with, and even dependent upon, teaching; and the kind that has no relation whatsoever to teaching except insofar as students may be easily and conveniently hired as technicians or assistants.

It is a fair generalization, I believe, that traditionally research was only undertaken in universities when it could be properly synchronized with a man's teaching responsibilities; more to the point, it was the kind of research—small in scale, personal, and flexible—that was almost indistinguishable from teaching, most notably at the graduate level. But today every major university, if only for reasons of revenue, covets large-scale research of endowed or contract character, and most of this, it appears, does not so easily lend itself to becoming the context of teaching-in-research. It could as well perhaps be carried on outside universities. But in magnitudes of tens of millions of dollars, it *is* carried on within universities, and the highly specialized, technical positions in which graduate students find themselves in these vast projects offer more in the way of financial income than in education.

## THE STRUCTURE OF GRADUATE WORK

This leads us to brief consideration of the relationship of the graduate student to the field of sociology today. This relationship is changing, and I can perhaps best indicate the direction of its change by first contrasting the humanities and natural sciences in their characteristic approaches to graduate study.

When a student begins graduate work in a field like chemistry, he does not, typically, "work up" broad fields of accumulated learning, represented by hierarchies of courses; he "works under" an established scientist who immediately becomes, as it were, master to the newly arrived apprentice. Closely related is the fact that the chemistry student's work, almost from the beginning, is research—actual research carried on with the master and perhaps one or two other faculty members. Such research leads not uncommonly to joint publication in professional journals. Admittedly, some comprehension of broad fields, gained through courses and revealed through examinations, is demanded in the sciences, but it is my observation that what is really important is the research itself that the chemistry student is carrying on under faculty members—whose own research, be it noted well, often would be impossible were it not for the graduate students who assist him.

Now contrast the experience of the student in the humanities. A graduate student in literature, for example, faces a notably different situation. In the first place, he is much less likely to select a department for graduate work merely in order to work under a single man—and generally wouldn't be allowed to, in the science sense, if he had. Whatever use a humanities faculty member may make of graduate students for his own research, it is different and minor by comparison with the use of graduate students made by scientists. In any event, the task that confronts the graduate student in English is not that of plunging into actual research, but that of working up fields of accumulated scholarship—as many as eight or nine, if foreign languages are counted—which involve a large number of set courses and seminars and almost limitless reading. The essential objective of the humanities student is mastery of individuals, of ages of thought, and of the associated scholarship. Given this distant objective, it is no wonder that the humanities student normally puts in twice or three times as many years in preparation for his qualifying examinations as does the science student. It is only after successful completion of these examinations that the graduate student will be allowed for the first time to select a dissertation topic and to begin research in a sense even remotely comparable to that done by the chemistry student from the very beginning of his graduate work.

A student in chemistry who made a really important discovery on a highly specialized problem during his first year (and this can happen) would be a long way indeed toward his doctorate. Such a student would live out his residence requirement, would continue his research, supplemented by a few essential courses, but it is safe to say that he would have it made. On the other hand, a graduate student in literature who by miracle (and miracle is the word considering the scholarship that must be mastered and the quite different values involved) achieved a brilliant breakthrough on a problem in the understanding or interpretation of a major literary figure or period would be admired, but I doubt that he would be either substantively or psychologically any farther along toward his doctorate than would a humanities student who had not made such a breakthrough.

I seek no invidious contrast here. I happen to admire the breadth that examination-tested mastery of fields of scholarship can produce, as I also admire creative literary scholarship. Neither need result in a mandarin psychology. And I am constantly impressed by the number of individuals in the humanities whose minds retain their cutting edge even after five to seven years of rigorous and galling preparation for examinations, and also manage, sometimes in an extraordinarily short time after the degree is conferred, to produce works of originality and brilliance—and oftentimes, additionally, imaginative writing of excellence. Similarly, I am well aware of the number of scientists whose early immersion in research as graduate students, at the expense of broad exposure to ideas and reading, can result by early middle age in, first, an undue narrowing and then in dull repetition of substantially the same research.

Where does the sociology graduate student fall today between the science and humanities patterns which I have described here at some length? Doubtless, in many departments, he is still slightly closer to the student in literature than he is to the student in chemistry. But, given some of the changes noted above in the importance of research, the format of research, the type of research chosen today by sociologists in the universities, and, following from all of this, the increasing dependency of research sociology upon staffs of cheap and readily available assistants, it is my belief that before very much longer the structure of graduate work in sociology will be very close indeed to that of chemistry.

The increasing dependence of sociological research

upon graduate students will doubtless widen the gulf that already exists between the sociological production in liberal arts colleges and that of universities.

## SOCIOLOGY'S STRUGGLE FOR STATUS

Now let us turn to a different aspect of our subject, one that is somewhat more historical in character but equally relevant to the present position of sociology. The following discussion is concerned with what may accurately be called sociology's struggle for status. Like the Alger hero of old, sociology reveals to us a face that was always honest but for a long time poor and at the very bottom of the social-academic ladder. A struggle for prestige and secure status has characterized all the non-classical academic disciplines in the modern world, but in none, I think, has the struggle been at once more galling and more actually directive than in the field of sociology. In both Europe and the United States the essential character and substance of sociology were for many years largely determined by its success in finding a distinctive niche in academic halls.

This was notable in late nineteenth-century Germany. Unlike England and even France to some extent, Germany focused its intellectual activity within the university. The enormous burst of scholarship that we find in Germany from about 1850 on is to be explained in very large part by the renaissance of the universities that had begun a generation earlier. The university was central and essential in German thought in the nineteenth century.

This was not at all the case in England. Until the final years of the nineteenth century most of what developed in the social sciences and modern history did so outside academic walls. Within the universities, if

we may judge from some of the comments of contemporaries—including the writers of the Parlia-
mentary Commission report on Oxford and Cambridge
—there was little interest in anything beyond classical
philology and its protection from the winds of mod-
ernism. New departures in thought, in either the social
or physical sciences, were not popular in the two great
universities, and one result was the astonishing amount
of scholarly work done outside. The sociologist Herbert
Spencer was as free of academic pressures as the
biologist Charles Darwin, the historian George Grote,
or the philosopher John Stuart Mill.

The point I wish to emphasize here is that the
character of the sociology that developed in England,
as contrasted with Germany, clearly shows the effect
of its non-academic context. Because it was conceived
and developed by individuals each responsible to no
one but himself, it could and did aspire toward being
the single science of society. There was never the
necessity of shaping, of adjusting, of tacking with the
academic winds in England in the nineteenth century,
for the great works were written by scholars who were
outside the universities and therefore not compelled to
obey any dictates other than those of their own means
and consciences. Only recently has sociology's struggle
for a place in the curriculum become manifest in English universities.

Until the last decade or two of the nineteenth
century, the situation in France was nearly identical
with that of England. There too sociology, beginning
with its epochal statement by Auguste Comte, was
almost exclusively a non-university discipline, and it
developed as a kind of master science, recognizing
nothing but itself in the study of society. Although
Comte had, as a young man, been an examiner in the
*École Polytechnique* and Frédéric Le Play had served

on the faculty of the school of mines, the sociological work of each was done entirely outside the academic world and was long unrecognized by it. The idea that sociology must be defined in its relationship to other social sciences was as lacking in both these men as it was in Spencer or Buckle.

Very different, however, were the conditions of scholarship in Germany. It was Germany, above any other European country, that was most to affect the foundations of university life in the United States, and it is important therefore to inquire into the role of sociology in the German university. In Germany, certainly by mid-century, philosophy, history, political science, and psychology were fairly clearly differentiated as academic disciplines, and, under the grant of "academic freedom" in Prussia by which the faculty alone were to be responsible for the formation of curriculum, it was inevitable that there would be something of the same diplomatic relationship among the disciplines represented in the university that had existed among the nation states for several centuries.

What was inevitable specifically was competition for status among the several specialized disciplines. The kind of freedom a Spencer, Buckle, Comte, or Le Play had in developing a single inclusive master science was unthinkable in Germany in any of the disciplines, for, since everything scholarly in Germany was, almost by definition, a university subject, there were always the rival disciplines to keep one in line. It was in Germany that the curricular differentiation and scholarly specialization which have been the hallmarks of the late nineteenth and twentieth century university first came significantly into being.

Thus, in addition to the general obstacles sociology faced in its development, it had some of a special kind in Germany. There was, first, the necessity of its becoming a university discipline if it was to enjoy popular prestige; and there was, second and following from this, the problem of its achieving a scope and method that would not seem to be transgressing upon such already established disciplines as law, history, political science, and economics.

Hence, German sociology, almost from the very beginning, was preoccupied with questions of self-definition and self-image; with problems of methodology, of scope, and of objective. Sociology manifested, after its first grudging acceptance in the university, a good many of the qualities we generally sum up in the term "marginality." Regarded by others in the academic hierarchy as a kind of interloper, as a threatening poacher, as, at best, a dubious rival, it was necessary for sociology to justify itself to the older disciplines. It could do this, obviously, only by proving that in sociology there lay an insight and method, a subject matter and objective, that no other existing discipline contained. It is thus not strange, given this environmental context, that so much of the work done by Tönnies, Weber, Simmel, Troeltsch, and others proves to have, on close examination, a self-consciousness that is not to be seen at all in England and hardly before Émile Durkheim in France. The German sociologist, perhaps like modern man in general in the twentieth century, was preoccupied by the questions, what am I, what is my true role, and what is my end in life.

Given the historical fact that the American university (which does not much precede 1890) looked to Germany for its curricular model, it is not strange that similar status strivings should have characterized the history of sociology in this country. Here too the fields of philosophy, economics, government, and history achieved positions of influence earliest, looking with a dark eye upon disciplines such as psychology and sociology that seemed to threaten their empires. Sociology, in this country, unlike the case of Germany or any other part of Europe, had in addition the special difficulty of distinguishing itself from the old social work courses that had been a part of almost every theological seminary. There was, finally, the complication of the vast intellectual influence of Spencer in this country, which made some of the earliest academic manifestations of sociology undistinguishable from ethnological schemes of social development and progress. What we see at the beginning of the century in American departments of sociology is almost invariably an unstable duality of social work and philosophy of social progress.

Two circumstances helped to transform this situation. There was, first, the internal pressure for sociology to assume a character that did not invite taunts and recriminations from the other disciplines ("organized smatter," "the science of left-overs," "all method and no subject" were a few). Second, there was the general exodus of American university scholars almost single-mindedly to the universities and institutes in Germany. Here, in addition to obtaining a highly superior conception of the mission of the university, it was possible for American sociologists to get a vivid picture of sociology as a special science, one that could be charged with neither imperialism, at one extreme, or social uplift, at the other. I am not unmindful of the influence of France on the thinking of such key figures as Charles H. Cooley and George Herbert Mead, but no one will challenge, I think, the assertion that it was the German example that did the most to remake the American college into a university and the example of German sociology that did the most to rescue American sociology from the Scylla of

social work and the Charybdis of social development-
mentalism.

## EARLY INFLUENCE OF THE TEXTBOOK

But whereas in Germany—and also France after Durkheim—curricular pressures could be seen resulting in
works of extraordinary scholarship in sociology, the
same was only rarely true at first in the United States.
What we find in American sociology—at first in
freshets, then in floods over the academic landscape—
are textbooks for beginning students. No doubt the
immense impact of mass education—a force unfaced
by European scholars—helps to explain this, for large
classes combined with small libraries meant a heavy
reliance on textbooks. The enormous emphasis
throughout American life at this time on self-helps to
intellectual improvement gave the textbook a significance in all fields that it rarely possessed in Europe.
In any event, what we see in American sociology is a
vogue of the textbook, especially the principles textbook, that was to last for a good many years and to
make it the predominant image of sociology for most
people until fairly recently. The textbook, to be sure,
had much the same vogue for many years in the other
disciplines, but these disciplines escaped it earlier,
and I do not think that in them the textbook ever had
quite the profound importance that it did in sociology
from roughly 1910 to 1940. During this period the
*typical* work of American sociology was the principles
textbook. There were some important exceptions: the
works of C. H. Cooley, W. I. Thomas, Robert S. Lynd,
P. I. Sorokin (whose coming to the United States in
the 1920's did so much to raise the intellectual level of
the discipline), and R. M. MacIver (whose original

*Society*, 1931, though often used as a textbook was an influential theoretical treatise). No doubt there are others. But the generality of American sociology is best expressed in the cynical observation of a university president of the time that whereas other faculty members wrote books, sociologists wrote textbooks.

In short, the textbook of *principles* was the American approach to the same problem that had confronted sociologists in Europe: that of justifying a place for sociology in the academic curriculum. But whereas the European sociologist met this problem with works of extraordinary scholarship and philosophical subtlety, the American was largely content with the textbook, with only an occasional published Ph.D. thesis to give indication that American sociology could be anything else. The combination of missionary zeal and textbook royalties could, of course, be a gratifying one. Like the missionaries who went to Hawaii, American sociologists set out to do good with their textbooks, and often ended up doing very well.

## SOCIOLOGY'S COMING OF AGE

It was, I suggest, the sociological renaissance beginning in the late 1930's that terminated alike academic insecurity and refuge in the principles textbook. And leading the renaissance, like Venice and Florence of old, were the two city-states of Harvard and Columbia. These two departments had the same magnitude of influence on the profession in the 40's and 50's that Chicago's great department had had in the 20's. It is interesting to note that behind all three eruptions of quality was the incorporation into new and specific areas of research of major ideas from the Europeans: Simmel preeminently at Chicago; Weber and Durkheim at Harvard and Columbia.

Today it would appear that curricular position exerts little if any real influence on the content and character of sociology. To a degree simply unknown a generation ago, the dominant tendencies in sociology today are reflections of incentives and pressures that go far beyond the curricular context; that go indeed, as we noted at the beginning of this paper, to the length and breadth of the profession and to all the areas—governmental, industrial, and professional—in which sociology is today involved. Pure research, rather than the predominantly teaching interests of curriculum, has decisive influence today in creating seed beds of new tendencies in sociology. Research and, of course, the incentives and imperatives of government and business.

One question might be asked in conclusion: To what extent will individual departments give color and direction to the profession in the future? It has been said by someone—by McGeorge Bundy, I believe—that the age of great-man presidents has been succeeded by great-man department chairmen. The only trouble with this attractive generalization is that, in the earlier history of American academic life, the two went together. In the same way that the great-man presidents like Harper, Angell, White, or Wheeler gave personality and direction to a whole university, the great-man chairmen like Giddings, Sumner, Small, Cooley, or Park gave personality and direction to a department. It may be argued, I believe, that the age of great-man presidents and great-man chairmen is being succeeded by great interlocking committees and, given incessant leaves of absence coupled with replacement professorships, interlocking departments and interlocking universities.

# (4)

# The Conventional Wisdom

# of Education and Sociology

＊

## MARVIN BRESSLER

"Nothing is more remarkable in the whole domain of sociology," a knowledgeable British colleague has observed, "than the recent elevation of station within it that the study of educational institutions has experienced." [1] This estimate and the situation it describes both seem just. The sociology of education has now earned the imprimatur of respectability but only after sociologists of substantial reputation and consequence had testified by their researches that they stood prepared to rescue the study of formal education from the desuetude that had befallen it as a result of historical neglect. The current proliferation of programmatic statements, surveys of the literature, and monographs produced by competent professionals lends

---

[1] A. Halsey, Book Review of Theodore Caplow and Reece J. McGee, *The Academic Marketplace* and Paul F. Lazarsfeld and Wagner Thielens, Jr., *The Academic Mind*, in *American Journal of Sociology*, 67 (September, 1961), p. 209.

credence to the prophetic gossip in the corridors that increasingly forecasts that education will be "the next *really* 'hot' field." [2]

Sociologists are not conspicuously more altruistic than other scholars and their recent lavish expenditure of energy on the study of education may be safely interpreted as primarily an attempt to advance their own science. As Orville Brim has noted, "For the sociologist, the formal educational system of this country constitutes what is probably his richest and most accessible natural source of raw data on personality and social interaction; it needs only to be systematically mined by careful research." [3] At the same time it is the basic assumption of this paper and the conceit of our discipline that the sociological analysis of education will prove beneficial not only to the observer but also to the observed.

Speaking broadly, sociology is potentially capable of making three fundamental contributions to educational theorists and practitioners: (1) by describing the impact of the external social system on the total educational process; (2) by providing systematic analyses of the school as a major institution in American society; and (3) by bringing sociological theory and method to bear on social interaction in the classroom setting.[4]

---

[2] For recent surveys of work in the sociology of education, see Orville G. Brim, Jr., *Sociology and the Field of Education*, Russell Sage Foundation, 1958; Neal Gross, "The Sociology of Education," R. K. Merton, L. Broom, and L. S. Cottrell, eds., *Sociology Today*, Basic Books, 1959, pp. 129-159; see also Special Issue on Sociology and Education, *Harvard Educational Review*, 29 (Fall, 1959). For a "Synopsis of Needed Educational Research" see supplement to Paul F. Lazarsfeld and Sam D. Sieber, "Organizational Problems of Educational Research" (hectographed).

[3] Brim, *op. cit.*, p. 7.

[4] Neal Gross, "Some Contributions of Sociology to the Field of Education," *Harvard Educational Review*, 29 (Fall, 1959, pp. 275-287.

It is true that sociological knowledge in these areas is currently meager and that the ascent of the sociology of education to the level of a mature social science must at present be regarded as a remote rather than an imminent goal. We shall argue, nevertheless, that the findings of a discipline do not exhaust its gifts, that scholars always say more than they explicitly intend, and that even broad sociological orientations may yield limited, but by no means minor, benefits to educationists.[5]

Both the sociologist and the educationist bring to the study of education a series of shared epistemological convictions, value perspectives, and prescriptions for action that together constitute a "party line" or in Galbraith's felicitous phrase, the "conventional wisdom" of the field.[6] The conventional wisdom of any

[5] The term "educationist" is used throughout this paper as a synonym for professor of education. It should not be necessary to add that the educationist pursues an honorable and hopefully an honored calling and that the term is used without pejorative intent.

[6] John Kenneth Galbraith, *The Affluent Society*, Houghton Mifflin, 1958. See early chapters. The term "conventional wisdom" as it is here employed is used in a less critical sense than Galbraith's usage. A more formal word, "ethos," as employed by anthropologists, has a certain kinship to the meaning which I am attaching to "conventional wisdom" in this paper. "Ethos is taken to mean the constellation of acquired drives or motivations which are characteristic of a culture, plus the goals, both explicit and implicit, toward which cultural activities are directed or upon which high value is placed." See John Gillin, "Ethos and Cultural Aspects of Personality," Sol Tax, ed., *Heritage of Conquest*, The Free Press, 1952.

Obviously, there is no monolithic unity in either education or sociology. The philosophic divisions in education are ordinarily identified as perennialism, essentialism, progressivism, and reconstructionism. At the risk of violating the subtleties of educational philosophy these schools may be thought to represent a continuum from emphasis on the past to emphasis on the present and the future; orientation toward the broad historical tradition of Western culture to orientation toward the be-field is a set of organized standard solutions to Kant's haunting queries: "What can I know? What should I do? What may I hope?" [7] It is established by a consensus that arises from assumption, knowledge, fiat, or desire and it is often dominated by a mood that is dogmatic, rigid, polemical, and partisan. It is a pure distillate minus bureaucratic realism and human frailty.

As sociologists of education expand their activities, conduct their researches, and publish their results they will perforce establish personal and professional contacts with professional educationists. In the ensuing dialogue the conventional wisdom of the two fields will collide. If this interchange is responsible, the minimum sociological offering would be an expanded range of intellectual alternatives and the minimum educationist response, a more self-conscious and articulate commitment to its own fixed positions. Under optimum conditions educationists might feel con-

---

havioral sciences; education as a means of transmitting societal values to education as a means of introducing social change; emphasis on intellectual rigor to emphasis on the whole person. See George F. Kneller, "Contemporary Educational Theories," George F. Kneller, ed., *Foundations of Education*, Wiley, 1963, pp. 92-132. The conflict between (1) perennialists and essentialists and (2) progressivists and reconstructionists is devoid of real bitterness. Although perennialists and essentialists have won the day in a number of states and cities they have negligible influence among contemporary educationists. For some recent works expressing their mood, see Arthur E. Bestor, *The Restoration of Learning*, Knopf, 1955; Albert Lynd, *Quackery in the Public School*, Little, Brown, 1953; Hyman G. Rickover, *Education and Freedom*, Dutton, 1959; and Mortimer B. Smith, *The Diminished Mind*, Regnery, 1954.

[7] "The whole interest of my reason, whether speculative or practical, is concentrated in the three following questions: What can I know? What should I do? What may I hope?" Immanuel Kant, *Critique of Pure Reason*, translated by F. Max Müller, Macmillan, 1900, pp. 645-646. These questions have been very liberally adapted in this paper and are used for heuristic purpose only.

strained to augment or revise cherished but inadequate tenets of their own conventional wisdom.

This thesis suggests that contact between thought systems may be conceived as a special case of the process of acculturation which in its most comprehensive form may be defined as "cultural change that is initiated by the conjunction of two or more autonomous cultural systems." [8] Change follows contact only when orthodoxy is confronted by alien, novel, or opposing tendencies. One task of analysis, then, is to juxtapose the contrasting and incongruent elements of the occupational roles and the conventional wisdom of education and sociology. Later we shall try to indicate the ways in which these seemingly antithetical thought systems are compatible and to specify the conditions for their collaboration. Since the professor of education and the university sociologist ordinarily define the situation for their colleagues elsewhere we shall confine our analysis to them. The ensuing discussion leans heavily on *Verstehen* and limited experience, and the hope that the study of acculturation of thought systems will soon yield monographs rather than impressionistic essays is here advanced with more than ritualistic seriousness.

## THE CONVENTIONAL WISDOM OF EDUCATION

In education, as elsewhere, thoughtways are seldom unmoved prime movers and doctrine tends to follow function. The educationist's response to Kant's questions are shaped throughout by the brute fact of mass education. The goal of mass education means that a

---

[8] Participants of the SSRC Summer Seminar on Acculturation, "Acculturation: An Exploratory Formulation," *American Anthropologist*, 56 (January-March, 1954), p. 974.

senior generation of professors places its intellectual
capital at the disposal of an intermediate generation of
prospective teachers for the sake of the putative needs
of a third generation consisting of all children and ado-
lescents. This definition of function governs the educationist's occupational ideology, tasks, and roles, and
markedly influences his intellectual approach, standards, and activities.

## What May I Hope? The Third Generation and the Ideology of Mass Education

Formal education is a vehicle of socialization, that is
to say, it is an agency that seeks to develop "in individuals . . . the commitments and capacities which
are essential prerequisites for their future role performances." [9] The distinctive challenge to mass education in a mass society lies in (1) the variety and complexity of social roles, (2) their problematic stability
over time, and (3) the great range of genetic endow-
ments and social characteristics that are represented
in the school population.

The fundamental tenets of the conventional wisdom
of education are necessarily directly addressed to these
three circumstances. Its basic propositions are: (1)
Formal education should develop cognitive skills, but
this task does not exhaust its responsibilities. The
school must train young people in all areas that cru-
cially affect role performance. (2) Social change can
be controlled by the application of disciplined intelligence. The educational process is the only alterna-
tive to social stagnation or revolutionary violence. It
is the duty of education to preside over gradualistic

---

[9] For a penetrating discussion of the socialization process in
the classroom, see Talcott Parsons, "The School Class as a
Social System: Some of Its Functions in American Society,"
*Harvard Educational Review*, 29 (Fall, 1959), pp. 297-318.

change toward a more perfect expression of the democratic tradition. (3) All young people are capable of individual growth, and when proper provisions are made for individual differences they can all benefit from education at some level.

It is obviously beyond the scope of this paper to treat extensively the diverse items of knowledge, assumption, or desire that comfort the educationist in his ideological position. However, it is possible to indicate some of the areas over which the conventional wisdom has established its hegemony and to identify its archetypical heroes. In social philosophy it prefers John Stuart Mill to Karl Marx; in contemporary political philosophy, Arthur Schlesinger, Jr., to William Buckley; in economics, John Maynard Keynes to Adam Smith; in sociology, Lester F. Ward to William Graham Sumner; on the role of intelligence, Bertrand Russell to Sören Kierkegaard; on the limits of free expression of opinion, Justice Black to Justice Frankfurter; on the basic influences of personality, Erich Fromm to Franz Kallman; on the plasticity of the personality, John Watson to William McDougall; in psychotherapy, Fredric Wertham to Nathan Kline; on the basic determinants of social problems, William Healy to Cesare Lombroso; on race differences, Otto Klineberg to Frank McGurk.

The conventional wisdom abstracts from the doctrines symbolized by the preferred names both a mood and an explanation for the human condition. The mood is informed by the image of man as victim and is sustained by the faith that he will prevail. Men are ravaged by disease, deceived by myth, corrupted by avarice, and degraded by poverty—but the message of man's fate is not despair but a vision. The ideology of mass education rejects the tragic view of life, for philosophy provides the promise and science the assurance that men can ascend the mountain if they but choose to do so together. The ethic of the ideology of mass education is therefore the Judaeo-Christian tradition, its love, forbearance, and compassion; its science is alive with options, with change, fluidity, and development.

The concepts that offend the educationist are from his perspective both immoral and false. He rejects words implying limits ("fixed," "immutable," "innate"); biological determination ("genetic," "hereditary," "instinct"); artificial differences ("white supremacy," "elite," "fit"); restrictions of rational discussion ("censorship," "mysticism," "authority"); violence ("revolution," "conflict," "force"). He despises the vocabulary of despair, for in the conventional wisdom of education truth and wish are one.

The credo of unlimited hope performs useful functions for education. For the professor or schoolman who sights the promise of individual and social salvation the school becomes a church and work a calling. In a profession where frustration and failure are common the ideology of mass education revives professional energy and protects children against the comfortable cynicism and apathy that might otherwise afflict their teachers.[10]

For these reasons educationists find it difficult to include these fundamental assumptions and doctrines of the conventional wisdom within the effective range of free inquiry. Faith and dogma do not suffer dissent gladly and genuine intellectual reservations are often greeted by the moral outrage that is properly reserved for heresy rather than error. Ironically, educationists who have been variously praised and blamed for shed-

---

[10] I am indebted to David Riesman for a stimulating discussion of this point. He is, of course, absolved from any responsibility for formulations in this paper.

ding the restraints of the past have responded to the
pressures of mass education by producing an orthodoxy that is no less rigid because it stems from a
newer tradition.

## What Should I Do? Developing Role Versatility in the Second Generation

Formal education includes the orderly transmission of
a body of knowledge, skills, and values under the
guidance of a teacher. In simple terms the professor
of education teaches prospective teachers how to
teach.[11] The conventional wisdom views the educationist as the precipitant of a chain reaction that grows
more powerful as it recedes in time. The professor is
agent as well as scholar, his students are middlemen
as well as consumers, and each is sensitive to the
sovereign principle, virtuous as it is malleable, of
"meeting individual and social needs." The stunt,
of course, is to discern the extensiveness, the intensity,
and the duration of "individual and social needs" and
to develop a standard for adjudicating their competing
demands. Even in the absence of consensus, however,
a familiar taxonomy of chapter headings provides a
classificatory scheme and calls the pedagogue to his
sense of duty. The initiate understands that in addition to his intellectual stewardship (and sometimes
in its stead) the adroit schoolman inculcates "desirable

---

[11] Educationists sometimes share the responsibility for content
preparation in academic subjects and also prepare students to
teach in areas that fall outside the purview of the liberal arts
college. Many of the atrocity stories dealing with undignified
courses in schools of education overlook the fact that their
curricula are necessarily responsive to the program of the lower
grades. An Albert Lynd may point to the large number of business education courses at one eastern university but manifestly
if children are to learn shorthand their teachers must know
Gregg from Pitman.

social values," stimulates "personality growth," and encourages pupils to "master their environment."

The stated desiderata that fall under these rubrics are customarily catalogued under appropriate headings, are assigned equal rank and weight, and are as wide in their range as they are unexceptionable in their merit. Admiral Rickover has noted that one such influential list of desired competencies includes: he "helps when necessary to eliminate insects and vermin which tend to carry germs"; she "wears with growing self-assurance appropriate foundation garments and clothing properly styled for the maturing figure"; he "stands for and defends the right of each individual to worship God in his own way or refrain from religious affiliations or beliefs." [12]

Such diffuse goals nevertheless define the direction of the educationist's strivings. His mandate to prepare his students to meet diverse needs places a premium on versatility and aggravates serious imbalances in the quality-quantity equation. As personnel and required competencies increase, the capacity of professors and teachers to perform their professional roles declines. The process of preparing teachers for multiple role performances necessarily dilutes the quality of instruction. Moreover, as William H. Whyte was not the first nor the last to show, future teachers are "those with the least aptitude for education of all Americans attending college" [13]—and this chronic situation is unlikely to change materially in the immediate future.

Education competes in the marketplace with other professions that can offer more lucrative rewards. As S. M. Lipset has suggested and experience confirms,

---

[12] Rickover, *op. cit.*, pp. 140-141.
[13] William H. Whyte, Jr., *The Organization Man,* Doubleday Anchor, 1957, p. 91.

professions such as education can seldom promise their novitiates a life of affluence.[14] In 1960 some 335 colleges and universities conferred 120,000 earned undergraduate and graduate degrees in education—too few for estimated needs and too many for any hope of excellence.[15] Given the facts of huge numbers, scarce talent, and limited rewards it is unrealistic to suppose that education will be able to recruit sizable proportions of students from the gifted end of the ability spectrum.

Many fine students do, of course, enter teaching. For example, Christopher Speeth, a young teacher in Philadelphia's Arthur Elementary School, mobilized college students and an entire slum community to assist him in his impeccable production of *Oedipus Rex* featuring an all-star cast of low-income Negro children.[16] But it is difficult to escape the conviction that although workshops on the Greek Tragedy and the Culturally Deprived Child may yet abound in the land, charismatic teachers will continue to be in short supply. Nor is it altogether clear that a sudden influx of genuinely capable students into teachers' colleges would be in the national interest. By what existing calculus can we determine the optimum allocation of brains and talent? Shall we try to increase the proportion of first-rate teachers at the expense of physics, mathematics, medicine, engineering, and social work —all professions that join in the plaintive chant, "We need more, we need better."

---

[14] See Seymour Martin Lipset, "American Intellectuals: Their Politics and Status," *Daedalus*, 88 (Summer, 1959), pp. 460-486.
[15] See Mary Irwin, ed., *American Universities and Colleges*, 8th edition, American Council on Education, 1960, p. 142; U.S. Bureau of the Census, *Statistical Abstract of the United States: 1961*, 82nd edition, 1961, pp. 130, 172.
[16] *Philadelphia Evening Bulletin*, August 29, 1962.

Under the circumstances the educationist must make
do with existing human materials but he must not
retreat from the ideal that requires him to train students to give an all-purpose education to all children.
Ideology aside, the teacher's prospects for engaging the
minds of large numbers of ill-equipped and poorly
motivated pupils, especially in urban areas, depend on
his mastery of the roles of Clinical Social Scientist and
Secular Priest as well as Guardian of the Intellect.

TRAINING THE CLINICAL SOCIAL SCIENTIST   Of all the behavioral sciences psychology has had the most influence on education. The educationist is especially eager
for his students to recognize and respect individual
differences in capacity and receptiveness to learning.
Hence education courses deal with the rudiments of
motivation, learning, and perception theory. They also
prepare students to recognize aberrant symptoma-
tology, to treat personality deviation as morally neu-
tral, and to proceed on the conviction that with the
optimum blend of "warmth" and "firmness" suffusing
the classroom, even the least likely candidate can be
salvaged for scholarship.

The conventional wisdom predisposes the educationist to think in idiographic rather than nomothetic
terms, to emphasize individual rather than statistical
lawfulness, and to show scant respect for actuarial
generalizations expressed as norms. "A person," says
the conventional wisdom, "is not a statistic." In his
concern for understanding idiosyncratic characteristics
the professor ordinarily instructs his students to prefer
the qualitative vocabulary of case analysis to the quantitative language of group description.

Sociological and anthropological orientations may be
introduced into education courses in the process of
identifying the broad social forces affecting education

and in the notion of "group dynamics." The student is subjected to the ritual of "group process" on the grounds that he will eventually preside over class discussions and participate in group decisions at the faculty level. The educationist, therefore, seeks to transform his students into committee personalities who neither wound nor are wounded and who do not impose their own intellectual passions on their fellows.

There arises among educationists and their students a form of bland exchange conducted according to a mannered etiquette of institutionalized tolerance. Interaction occurs at several levels of awareness and the search for truth is circumscribed by an anxiety not to offend, to appear dogmatic, or to seem intransigent. In such intercourse the nuances are often more vivid than the content, implications overwhelm assertions, and group process occasionally becomes a caricature. Everyone speaks in interrogatories (Would there be any value in adding a non-credit typing course? Or is there not a limited sense in which it might be said that under certain conditions . . . ?) and the entire proceedings resemble a group therapy session composed entirely of guidance counsellors all using the non-directive technique.

TRAINING THE SECULAR PRIEST  The major task of the professor in training the Secular Priest is to remind his students of the ubiquity of value considerations even in the most seemingly trivial aspects of the educational process. An anecdote, not wholly apocryphal, may serve as an illustration. A graduate seminar in Problems of the Modern High School is playing Show and Tell. Each teacher reports in sequence on "co-curricular" (emphatically *not* "extra-curricular") activities in the high schools of Larchmont and Willowood and North Winsbury. These are veteran students

who are sensitive to the aesthetics of concept formation and cannot be provoked into committing any
semantic gaffes. "Extra-curricular" has the implication
of superfluous but the dramatic club "encourages self-
expression" and self-expression is a need.

A teacher from Tanglehorne High School reports
that "our system" will soon build a swimming pool,
and he thinks that it is not too early to start pondering
the challenge this offers for the co-curricular program.
He wonders what the class thinks is the *primary* objective of a swimming club. The class cynic, proud and
defiant, answers that the purpose obviously is to teach
the kids to swim. The students laugh tolerantly—every
class needs its rebel and there will be time enough to
convert vanity into prayer. Someone else says that for
the sake of getting the ball rolling he will say that a
swimming club is a dandy way to develop habits of
water safety. The professor speaks. The previous suggestion has made him a mite uncomfortable because
at some intuitive level he cannot quite define, he
rather feels that water safety is a secondary aim; and
besides, is "habits" the proper word in this context?

The discussion continues and the professor, Socrates
in modern dress, stings, detects a paradox, demands
clarification, but is gentle withal. At length, the seminar reaches a meeting of the minds. "The swimming
club should be an integral part of the recreational division of the co-curricular program whose major purpose
should be the development of democratic principles
of individuality and democratic practices of coopera-
tion during leisure time activities."

TRAINING THE GUARDIAN OF THE INTELLECT    The educationist prepares his students to play the role of the
Guardian of the Intellect on the assumption that disciplined intelligence is man's last hope, his only instru-

ment for mastering the present and for anticipating
and controlling the future. The educationist is an intellectual puritan who is profoundly serious about the
use of the mind. He respects ideas almost to the point
of reverence but he never finds them beautiful.
Thoughts solve problems or they do not, and he cannot be distracted by the merely erudite, elegant, or
wise.

Accordingly, the educationist is much occupied in
transmitting to his students durable, all-purpose prob-
lem-solving techniques and orientations that are presumably relevant for a variety of contingencies. These
may be employed by the prospective teacher and,
when suitably modified, by his pupils. The student is
encouraged to "think critically" about man, society,
and the educational system. "Critical thinking" is
taught in education courses without recourse to formal
logic and consists primarily of speculative exercises
on the intended and unintended consequences of al-
ternative courses of action.

The ultimate arbiter of disputes raised by the process of critical thinking is *the* scientific method as the
educationist understood it in the days of his youth.
Science is the source of knowledge and the controlled
experiment is science. Truth is accessible, if at all,
through the "steps" that begin comfortingly with the
"statement of the problem" and end with "revise the
hypothesis to fit the data." [17] The difficulty is, of course,

---

[17] Conant's comments on the "steps" are instructive. See James
B. Conant, *Modern Science and Modern Man*, Doubleday
Anchor, 1954, pp. 46-47. "What is often defined as the scientific method is nothing more or less than an approximate description of a well-ordered systematized empirical inquiry. Now,
systematized or well-ordered empirical inquiries are one element in the advance of science; the other element is the use of
new concepts, new conceptual schemes that serve as working
hypotheses on a grand scale. Only by the introduction of a
theoretical element can the degree of empiricism be reduced."

that the ritual of the "steps" provides no hint of the impact of the grand-scale hypotheses of the physical sciences, the revolution in data-processing logic and procedure, the leap forward in mathematics, new approaches to concept and theory formation, recent developments in the logic of formal inference, improvements in scale construction, or advances in the techniques of multivariate analysis.

It is understandable why recent developments in science and philosophy have had little impact on the educationist. The proliferation of knowledge and the increasing sophistication of technique in philosophy and the social sciences challenge the industry of the specialist and are the amateur's despair.[18] The fact remains that although the logic of experimental design is a triumph of science, it does provide a rather narrow base from which to view the world. The man so situated will learn little from contemporary social science and even less from philosophy.

These considerations mean that for the educationist science is an honored symbol but experience becomes the actual basis for knowledge. He has lived, he has taught, he has observed teachers, he has served in school systems, and he knows what he knows. If you treat people as human beings their morale will be good because that is the way it happened in Larchmont. It is in this sense that a diluted pragmatism becomes part of the educationist doctrine. An idea is true because it connects with experience, because it

---

[18] The scientific journal was invented in the mid-seventeenth century. Prince reports that "If we make . . . a count extending in the time from 1665 to the present day, it is immediately obvious that the enormous increase in the population of scientific periodicals has proceeded from unity to the order of a hundred thousand with an extraordinary regularity seldom seen in any man made or natural statistic." See Derek J. de Solla Prince, *Science Since Babylon,* Yale University Press, 1961, p. 96.

simplifies complexity, and because it saves intellectual labor. However, the rigor of the proof *in extenso* would be unsatisfactory to Peirce, James, or Dewey. *Intuition* promises that a vaguely defined "it" will "work" in Larchmont; casual *experience* verifies that it did; *plausibility* offers a "common sense" explanation for its efficiency; *confidence* extends the finding to Willowood; and virtue assures us that as everybody knows, decency ought to and therefore does triumph.

## What Can I Know? The Professional Roles of the First Generation

Like other academicians, the educationist is potentially cast in triple roles: the scholar who acquires knowledge, the teacher who is responsible for its transmission, and the researcher who is responsible for its extension. Education is a synthetic, applied, and normative discipline, characteristics that strongly affect the manner in which the professor performs his various roles.

THE EDUCATIONIST AS SCHOLAR OR THE GENERALIST-TRANSLATOR Educationists generally agree that pedagogy that aspires to become science must consist of an organized set of philosophically valid goals and practices which are compatible with the findings of the behavioral sciences and are applicable to concrete learning situations. Education so conceived must abandon all pretensions of self-determination and become the acknowledged debtor of philosophy, psychology, anthropology, and sociology. The need for someone to digest, summarize, and interpret this mass of materials compiled by specialists in other disciplines gives rise to the role of the generalist-translator. The first duty of the competent professor of education is to become conversant with the principles of formal science, axiology, and epistemology; with the mechanisms of motivation, perception, and learning; with culture, social structure, process and function. Viewed from this neo-Comtean perspective education is located near the apex of the hierarchy of human studies and is surely one of the most formidable of intellectual pursuits.

But for the educationist, synthesis is not enough; knowledge must be transformed from an ornament into a tool. An idea is treasured for its consequences; it must be exportable, and the pay-off comes when real teachers confront real children in a concrete learning situation. The translator's task is complicated by the fact that any educational program designed for the young is in part a wager about tomorrow and contains hidden predictions whose accuracy cannot be assessed for decades. In view of the complexity of personality and the rapidity of social change, the educationist is understandably a trembling prophet. His reputation for fuzziness is often no more than a prudent suspicion of specific substantive findings and the legitimate fear of premature closure. The translator must, therefore, possess sufficient intellectual taste and agility to avoid the fallacy of misplaced concreteness even as he struggles to convert recondite knowledge into meaningful educational terms.

The dilemma of the generalist-translator is measured by the awesome distance between the requirements of his role and the actuality of his talents. He is alas, not da Vinci, but an ordinary man. Moreover, the role occupant seldom qualifies for his task by meeting formal eligibility requirements. Indeed, he is ordinarily free of all save the most innocent involvement with any of the foundation disciplines he proposes to synthesize and apply. Hence the much admired "expansion of horizons" may sensitize the educationist to

the great range of variables, hypotheses, and assertions
that must in some fashion be incorporated into a viable
program of teacher education, but he is more likely to
become conversant with the rhetoric of scientific discourse than with its substance.

THE EDUCATIONIST AS TEACHER    The educationist is a
trustee of an intellectual legacy; but he is energized
not so much by a passion for new treasure as by the
moral compulsion to distribute his hoard. He is, after
all, a professor in a teacher training institution and his
*raison d'être* is his presumed expertise in teaching
others to improve the quality of their instruction. An
elementary respect for moral nicety requires him to be
no less zealous than his students. His own methods of
teaching must be imaginative and diversified, his manner amiable, his social concern manifest, and his control of classroom atmosphere exquisite. The educationist, then, is thus greatly occupied with class prepara-
tions, retrospective evaluations, joint planning sessions,
and individual conferences with students to a degree
undreamt of in the philosophy of other university professors. Since the educationist, like other mortals, must
purchase time and energy for one activity at the expense of others, his attention is necessarily deflected
from other functions, including personal growth and
research.

THE EDUCATIONIST AS RESEARCHER    It is noteworthy
that in American institutions of higher learning where
research leads to publication, publication to honor, and
honor to tangible reward, the educationist shows so
little inclination to extend the knowledge in his field.
The status of research in schools of education is well
summarized by Eric Gardner: "Very few Master's can-
didates make any substantial attempt at becoming
either producers or consumers of research. Research is

still considered an important part of doctoral work and nearly every institution requires a doctoral dissertation. In general, faculty members make an occasional contribution." [19]

One reason for this situation is that it is extraordinarily difficult for practitioners of a synthetic and applied discipline to do competent research. Since the educationist has little specialized knowledge of the foundation disciplines and only perfunctory training in the logic and techniques of inquiry, he could scarcely excel in social, psychological, or philosophical investigation even if he were so inclined. Moreover, his action orientation leads him to excessive impatience with the time lag between a finding and its incorporation into practice. The research impulse suffers in education from lack of sympathy for the frivolous motive of curiosity.

In sum: for the conventional wisdom of education hope, knowledge, and duty constitute a coherent system. The extension of the Judeo-Christian tradition and the liberal ethic is the substance of our dreams, science tells us that our dreams are not extravagant, and education is an instrument that helps bring them into being. In following this conception, the educationist prepares students for multiple role performances, and as a generalist-translator he seeks implica-

---

[19] Eric F. Gardner, *Tomorrow's Graduate School of Education,* Syracuse University Press, 1958, p. 38.

Myron Lieberman observes: "How much money ought to be spent on educational research? Public education is a $15,000,-000,000 enterprise. Enlightened practice in large-scale industry and government is to spend 3 to 6 per cent of the total budget for research. In education, this would call for an expenditure of from $450,000,000 to $900,000,000 annually. In fact, it is unlikely that the country is spending more than $25,000,000 a year from all sources for educational research." See Myron Lieberman, *The Future of Public Education,* University of Chicago Press, 1960, p. 43.

tions for practice from among an embarrassment of riches—in the absence of specialized knowledge and a research tradition.

## THE CONVENTIONAL WISDOM OF SOCIOLGY

The professor of sociology who studies education is in the words of A. H. Halsey one of a "new generation of intensely professional sociologists determined to analyze education in the same terms and with the same methods used in the study of other social institutions." [20] The key phrases in this assessment explain much about the conventional wisdom of sociology. "Intensely professional" means that unlike the educationist, the sociology professor tends to think of social research as his true vocation and teaching as an ancillary burden. This orientation has both sacred and profane origins. Scholars who find joy in the process of discovery tend to be jealous of the time that is lost in assuring freshmen that when the sociologist says "culture" he does not really mean grand opera. But it is also true that the pure research impulse is reinforced by the initial process of professional socialization and by the reward system of the College of Arts and Sciences.

As one of its latent functions, graduate instruction conveys the message that it is somewhat *gauche* to invest too much energy or ego in classroom performance. Graduate professors teach this lesson indirectly by maintaining an invincible silence on pedagogical matters. An especially venturesome doctoral candidate who realizes that most of his working life will be spent in the academy and openly elects courses in educational methodology risks the censure of his peers.

---

[20] Halsey, *op. cit.*, p. 209.

Later, the new assistant professor will absorb the guild belief that constructing useful definitions and measures of good teaching is somehow beyond human ingenuity and that classroom visits by superiors are indelicate intrusions on the privacy of teacher and student. When all teachers are invisible all are equal, and length of bibliography may well become the sole criterion of productivity.

If "intensely professional" has a clear meaning to most sociologists, the nature of the appropriate "terms" and "methods" to which Halsey alludes is a matter of controversy. It is true that the boundaries of sociology are fixed for all its practitioners by the customary division of labor within the social sciences. Its domain is patterned social behavior rather than idiosyncratic occurrences. It focuses on differences between groups, aggregates, or categories and since these are the basic units of sociology, similarities among the individuals who comprise them must be assumed or demonstrated. Sociologists are especially mindful of the first two elements in Clyde Kluckhohn and H. A. Murray's classification of man: "Every man is in certain respects (a) like all other men, (b) like some other men, (c) like no other man." [21]

The conventional wisdom is further unified by the common recognition of the complexity of the social system. "Social" connotes interaction and "system" implies interrelatedness, so that activity of any of the parts of larger wholes has endless ramifications. Sociologists are ever alert to the danger that in the social universe there is sometimes more and sometimes less than meets the eye. Defenses against simplistic thinking are built into the conceptual apparatus of sociol-

---

[21] Clyde Kluckhohn and Henry A. Murray, "The Shaping of the Individual," Kluckhohn and Murray, eds., *Personality in Nature, Society, and Culture*, Knopf, 1948, p. 35.

ogy. It includes such polarities as functions and dysfunctions, manifest and latent functions, intended and unintended consequences, formal and informal structures, overt and covert behavior—all of which distinguish between the partial and complete, the apparent and real, the visible and hidden.

The oppressive awareness of complexity also has consequences for research strategy. The most obvious is that it exerts pressures on sociologists to increase their sensitivity to the conditions that are required to confirm or disconfirm propositions. The application of controls, the careful sifting of evidence, the diligent search for contrary instances have become routine requirements of sociological scholarship. At the same time sociology does not pretend to treat social phenomena in all of their concrete aspects and interrelationships. It uses theoretical constructs such as ideal types that deliberately falsify empirical reality and operational definitions and indices that violate conceptual purity. It has, moreover, largely abandoned the quest for universal generalizations that are always applicable to the class to which they refer. Sociologists are quite content to establish uniformities with a high probability of occurrence.

This much at least sociologists have in common. Their differences arise out of loyalty to one of three competing schools within the field. An elaboration of these ideal-typical approaches which may be termed Science, Action, and Significance is not possible in this essay but their salient characteristics are summarized in the diagram on the following page.[22]

_____

[22] For an extended account of divisions within the field of sociology, see Marvin Bressler, "Some Selected Aspects of American Sociology, September 1959 to December 1960," *The Annals of the American Academy of Political and Social Science*, 337 (September, 1961), pp. 146-159.

| | SCIENCE | | ACTION | SIGNIFI-CANCE |
|---|---|---|---|---|
| | Theory | Empirical Research | | |
| Role Model | Natural Scientist | | Engineer | European Intellectual |
| Primary Goal | Social Knowledge | | Solution of Social Problems | Social Criticism |
| Value Perspective | Ethically Neutral | | Guided by Dominant American Value Orientations | Challenges Dominant American Value Orientations |
| Criterion for Problem Selection | Theoretical Importance | | Social Importance of Segmental Problems | Social Importance of Fundamental Issues |
| Theoretical Perspective | Functionalism | | Pragmatic Liberalism | Humanism |
| Methodology | Logic and Mathematics | Rigorous Statistical Analysis | Statistical and Qualitative Analysis | Disciplined Insight |
| Criteria of Adequacy | Coherence | Correspondence | Usefulness | Perceptiveness |
| Intellectual Product | Analytical Schemes | Empirical Generalizations | Implications for Action | General Trends and Tendencies |

## What Can I Know?

All schools of American sociology believe that we do not know enough, but this view is held at various levels of conviction. The Actionist is relatively sanguine. He is persuaded that his one oft-repeated thesis has been sustained: (1) democratic and humane values should guide every aspect of American life; (2) these are honored more in the breach than in the observance in

segmental areas of experience (for example, racial discrimination, capital punishment, urban planning); (3)
action is needed to narrow the gap between official
values and situational reality. Since even crude scholarship can establish the presence of gross disparities
between reality and the American Creed, the Actionist
is frequently impatient with what he regards as unnecessary demands for greater methodological and
theoretical refinement.

The man of Significance is much less confident that
the social world is knowable. His universe consists of
the large issues that bedevil Western society: the rec-
onciliation of freedom and order, liberty and security,
quality and quantity, conformity and autonomy. And
since he wishes to understand these in all their complexity he must face continuity and change and his
gaze must transcend national boundaries. Thus the
authors of *The Lonely Crowd* tell us that they sought
to "interpret and organize our experience of contemporary America and its relation to the past and prospective future" and they apologize because "we
looked too much at our own country and too little at
the world." [23] In short, men of Significance "think big."

The penalty of intellectual ambition is that it considerably reduces the prospect of achieving reasonable
certainty. Contemporary theory borrowed from Scientific sociology provides scant guidance—structural
functionalism is essentially an analytic scheme, not a
theory of society. Marxism, Freudianism, or liberalism
in their orthodox forms are at the very least in need
of revisionist tempering. Moreover, from the stand-

---

[23] David Riesman, Nathan Glazer, and Reuel Denney, *The
Lonely Crowd,* Doubleday Anchor, 1953, p. 5; David Riesman
with the collaboration of Nathan Glazer, "*The Lonely Crowd:*
A Reconsideration in 1960"; Seymour Martin Lipset and Leo
Lowenthal, eds., *Culture and Social Character,* The Free Press,
1961, p. 420.

point of technical scholarship Significant sociology is frustrated because it can make only limited use of precise tools of empirical inquiry. These are clearly inappropriate if, as C. Wright Mills says, "when most social scientists come seriously to examine a significant problem, they find it most difficult to formulate in terms of any unit smaller than the nation state." [24] Robert K. Merton well describes the plight of Significant sociology when he refers to those who "do not know whether what we say is true, but it is at least significant." [25]

Scientific sociology is equally ambitious and perhaps even more troubled. Its ultimate goal is to fashion theories of social behavior that have the elegance and power of theory in the natural sciences. It should codify known empirical generalizations and sensitize the investigator to gaps in existing knowledge. At the point of its most comprehensive development it should be capable of generating still other theories by means of logical derivation. An aspiration of this magnitude requires Scientific sociologists to be mindful of the need for improvement in techniques of data collection, the logic of procedure, and the canons of formal science. Since sociologists have not been conspicuously successful in creating behavior theory, metasociology remains a major obsession of the field. The conventional wisdom of Scientific sociology holds that it is premature to consider "significant" problems. Its major sources of pride are its austerity, tough-mindedness, skepticism, and ethical neutrality.

The epistemology that sustains this emphasis is eclectic and generally innocent of philosophic sophistica-

---

[24] C. Wright Mills, *The Sociological Imagination*, Oxford University Press, 1959, p. 136.
[25] Robert K. Merton, "The Bearing of Sociological Theory on Empirical Research," *Social Theory and Social Structure*, The Free Press, 1957, p. 85.

tion. It is unified by a mood of mixed austerity and irreverence. The Scientific mood distrusts metaphysics, tradition, dilettantism, and passion. It is not surprising, therefore, that Scientific sociology finds the spirit of logical positivism especially congenial and several of its methodological dicta instructive. Logical positivism assaults metaphysics by rigorously defining the limits of fruitful inquiry; it scoffs at tradition by asserting that orthodox philosophy has been consistently detoured by meaningless questions; it eliminates dilettantism by requiring that its votaries master mathematics and symbolic logic; and it destroys passion by voluntarily abandoning the validation of values as a proper area of philosophical investigation. Moreover, logical positivism provides impressive philosophic support for the favorite sociological principle of induction and exerts pressures for confirming propositions by referring them to evidential data.

The Actionists, then, most nearly resemble the educationists in their feeling that most useful knowledge is known or at least knowable. The conventional wisdom of the other schools by contrast implies that now and in the immediate future sociologists will probably be obliged to settle for a level of achievement that is well below the threshold of scientific certainty.

## What May I Hope? What Should I Do?

Hope and duty have meaning for both sociology and society. For all schools hope is the desire that the study of society shall become a mature discipline; duty is the commitment to hasten its achievement. The schools differ, however, on their estimate of society's capacity to overcome its problems and on the responsibility of sociologists to participate in finding solutions.

Action sociologists are the social Calvinists of the behavioral sciences. On occasion they appear to have

overlearned a paraphrase of Santayana's mock syllo-
gism on sin: evil exists, evil is social, social evil can be
remedied, is it not wonderful that social evil exists so
that it can be remedied. Poverty, sickness, discrimination, injustice outrage their consciences and they seek
to transform the House of Intellect into the House
Militant. In this respect also Actionists and educationists are intellectual kinsmen. The crucial difference between them is that the Actionist seriously believes in
empirical research as an instrument of enlightened
social policy and his manifestoes are appended to detailed monographs. His hope is that "the facts" will
help persuade rational men to seek social justice; his
felt duty is to join the comfortable world of academia
to the public arena of struggle and decision.

The man of Significance lacks the buoyancy of the
Actionist because he has less faith in the ordinary social nostrums—education, legislation, the expenditure
of resources. His conventional wisdom restricts hope
because the issues that engage him cannot be extri-
cated from the web of history. Consider, for example,
the portrait of modern man as he is depicted in Riesman's "other-directed personality," Whyte's "organization man," and Mills' "Cheerful Robot." The common
meaning of these typologies is that the American is
"passive and joyless" and "obedient to unsatisfying
values." [26] He is over-integrated into his group, too
responsive to its goals, and too sensitive to the estimate
of his peers. In short, he lacks a sense of self; he is as
others desire him.

If we are not content to cry havoc, we shall find
ourselves trying to reverse many of the major trends of
recent American history: the emergence of the garrison
state, technological advance, relative material abun-
dance, changes in the stratification profile, and the

---

[26] Riesman with the collaboration of Glazer, *op. cit.*, p. 445.

triumph of large-scale organization. Some of these we cherish and others are quite beyond our influence. It is no wonder that the redoubtable Mills confessed that he did not know the answer "to the cultural and political question of the Cheerful Robot," [27] or that Riesman acknowledges that his suggestions for developing a more autonomous social character "have been paltry ones," [28] or that Whyte is finally reduced to urging job applicants to give false responses to personality tests.[29]

From the standpoint of the Significance sociologists the probability that the world may not be manageable is insufficient reason for surrender. Their conception of duty is clearly expressed by Mills. "But is it not clear that no answers will be found unless these problems are at least confronted? Is it not obvious that the ones to confront them, above all others, are the social scientists of rich societies? That many of them do not now do so is surely the greatest human default being committed by privileged men in our times." [30]

The school of Science has resisted Mills' appeal with no apparent difficulty. As Alvin Gouldner has recently pointed out, "Today, all the powers of sociology from Parsons to Lundberg have entered into a tacit alliance to bind us to a dogma that 'Thou shalt not commit a value judgment,' especially as sociologists." [31] In the absence of an official stance on individual and social welfare, questions of hope and duty in the social realm are simply irrelevant. This view deserves special attention since, as judged by such criteria as acceptability to the establishment, scholarly prestige, and the cur-

[27] Mills, *op. cit.*, p. 176.
[28] Riesman, Glazer, and Denney, *op. cit.*, p. 346.
[29] Whyte, *op. cit.*, p. 22.
[30] Mills, *op. cit.*, p. 176.
[31] Alvin W. Gouldner, "Anti-Minotaur: The Myth of a Value-Free Sociology," *Social Problems*, 9 (April, 1962), p. 199.

rent emphases in graduate training, the school of Science appears to be dominant in the United States.

The conventional wisdom of sociology offers no unified message on man's fate or the social scientist's obligation. The Scientists will not consider the entire matter, Actionists are both hopeful and socially responsible, and Significant sociology is *engagé* despite its pessimism about the prospects of the human condition.

### THE USES OF SOCIOLOGY

The preceding highly selective account of the occupational roles and the conventional wisdom of education and sociology has largely ignored their similarities and emphasized their contrasting and incongruent elements. The purpose of this exercise was to discover whether these role and thought systems were essentially complementary or antagonistic. They would be compatible if, as the ensuing paragraphs purport to show, educationists could profitably incorporate some of the diverse elements of the conventional wisdom of sociology.

Sociology could enrich the educationist's conventional wisdom by expanding the range of its variables and concepts. The eye of the student that beholds the school is not innocent; it has been sensitized by the life styles, the modes of behavior, values and norms of his own particular social group. The counterpart of the psychologist's caveat "that every individual is different" is the sociologist's warning that the educator ignores systematic group differences at his peril.

The incorporation of these fundamental sociological assumptions into the conventional wisdom of education would in no way compromise its idiographic and clinical emphasis. Indeed sociological orientations could further specify structured sources of individual differences. Moreover, sociology can perform a useful screening function by identifying the statistically prominent characteristics in given populations that stimulate or impede learning. To cite only one example, Herbert Hyman has presented persuasive evidence that "reduced striving for success among the lower classes, an awareness of lack of opportunity, and a lack of valuation of education may hamper such persons in their school performances." [32] A teacher who is sensitive to these patterned differences should be better able to locate pupils who need specialized individual attention.

The educationist could also benefit from Scientific sociology's comparative tough-mindedness and from its self-conscious attention to problems of methodology and theory construction. The student whose knowledge is mainly derived from a relatively casual process of "critical thinking" may value his knowledge too highly, and because he lacks the training to graft new information on to a more inclusive body of systematic theory and empirical research, much of what he believes and practices may soon become tenuous and irrelevant. More generally, the field of education stands in need of the disinterestedness that characterizes the scientific mood. The provisional character of sociological wisdom might challenge the spirit of orthodoxy and stimulate a re-examination of educational theory and application. Sociology's sense of complexity, its consciousness of the frailty of current knowledge, its glorification of the scholar, the value-disengagement of its dominant school, all militate against a dogmatic adherence to fixed positions. The first step toward

---

[32] Herbert Hyman, "The Value Systems of Different Classes: A Social Psychological Contribution to the Analysis of Stratification," R. Bendix and S. M. Lipset, eds., *Class, Status, and Power*, The Free Press, 1953, pp. 426-442.

reform is to treat as problematic what has previously been regarded as established truth.

The conventional wisdom of education is not altogether free to adopt the rigorous and dispassionate spirit of science because of an unspoken fear that some findings may prove embarrassing to its ideological position and its conceptions of hope and duty. Indeed, one valuable property of sociological scholarship is that it *does* try to specify what values are actually threatened and what are probable outcomes and future trends. But although the findings of social research may mislead by incorrectly defining the outer limits of hope and the difficulties of duty they cannot demolish basic value premises.

A case in point is the antagonism of educationists to any suggestion that differential social achievements of whites and Negroes are partially determined by their inherent biological properties. The intense hostility to the concept of innate racial differences is more than routine rejection of faulty evidence. It is partially nourished by the belief that any scientific support for the doctrine of white supremacy questions the validity of egalitarian racial values. Ironically, this position has a certain kinship to the segregationist's demand that Negroes must "earn" full citizenship. It implies that intrinsic racial equality is one of the necessary preconditions for Negro emancipation. By so doing, it imposes tasks on social science that disinterested scholarship is not equipped to perform.

The "facts" are clear enough: average scores are lower for Negroes than for whites in most measurable "desirable" characteristics. However, a prime condition of useful social research—the control of potentially disturbing variables—can in this area neither be met nor approximated. Environmental deprivation and serious measurement error always introduce ambiguities

in the interpretation of racial differences. Under optimum circumstances "true" findings might (a) confirm
white superiority, (b) indicate contraction or disap-
pearance of existing differentials, or (c) reveal Negro
superiority. On purely logical as opposed to psychological grounds it is difficult to see how any of these
speculations on innate racial differences could prove
embarrassing to the educationist position. What, for
example, would be the ethical consequence of accept-
ing at face value the usual finding that only about one-
fourth of all Negroes reach the white median in I.Q.?
It would then follow that despite overlap in the curves
of intelligence of the two races, proportionately fewer
Negro students could meet college entrance requirements. But a general expectation of this sort would
hardly justify Governor Ross Barnett's efforts to bar
the demonstrably eligible James Meredith from admis-
sion to the University of Mississippi.

The Negro claim to equal educational opportunity
is beyond assault by differential test scores. The educationist ethic properly rests on principle or necessity,
not correlational determinism.[33] Empirical sociology
need not ratify and cannot nullify a fundamental conviction that the basic privileges and amenities of civilized existence should be accessible to all mankind.

A recitation of sociology's exemplary merits and the
contention that "inconvenient" findings in sensitive
areas are compatible with liberal values are of course
no assurance that sociology will actually succeed in
modifying the conventional wisdom of education. The

---

[33] It is often assumed that the dissemination of the belief in
the biological equality of all races is a tactical requirement in
the struggle for civil rights. This proposition is at least arguable.
Is it more effective to tell bigots (1) that science does not
confirm prejudiced observations, or (2) your views on racial
inequality are irrelevant to discussions about human freedom?

study of the acculturation of thought systems is a poorly developed field in the sociology of knowledge and there are few signposts to guide our anticipations. Fortunately, in Patricia Sexton's valuable book, *Education and Income*,[34] we have an instructive instance of recent sociological research that has been extraordinarily well received by educationists. An examination of this work may be helpful in identifying the characteristics of contemporary sociology that are most readily exportable.

Sexton's most general purpose is to demonstrate that the American system of education violates the "greatest of all democratic dreams—equal educational opportunity for all, without regard to race, religion or status." The author is able to report with pardonable pride that hers was the "first *study* of its kind." [35] Her methodology is unpretentious and relies almost exclusively on the comparison of scores and percentages but it is applied to "all relevant and available facts about the 285,000 students, 10,000 teachers, and almost 300 schools in [Detroit]." [36] The outcome of this prodigious labor is that Sexton establishes her major empirical generalizations beyond the possibility of cavil.

Sexton finds that in the schools of Detroit the school system magnifies the inequities of a stratified society by offering children of the "elite" "superior educational services of every variety" while denying them to the "underprivileged and culturally deprived." [37] The direct consequence is that children from low-income homes are overrepresented in the delinquent population and among those who score low in tests of

---

[34] Patricia Cayo Sexton, *Education and Income,* Viking Press, 1961, p. xx.
[35] *Ibid.*
[36] *Ibid.,* p. 20.
[37] *Ibid.,* p. xvii.

scholastic aptitude, reading, and intelligence. For the individual the result is deflation of self, anxiety, and hostility. At the societal level, lack of equal educational opportunity restricts the discovery of talent, contributes to working-class anti-intellectualism, and injures the competitive position of the United States *vis à vis* the Soviet Union.

All this greatly troubles Professor Sexton and she responds with more than forty prescriptions for action. These vary in specificity but are uniformly in the imperative mood. They include such staple items as "more attention should be given to the psychological, medical, and nutritional needs of lower income students . . ." and "class size in lower income schools should be reduced"; inoffensive proposals urging that "ways of stimulating 'school spirit' on lower income students should be worked out"; and the controversial demand that since standard measures of intelligence are class biased the "use of I.Q. tests should be stopped." [38]

The high repute enjoyed by *Education and Income* in educationist circles is partially attributable to its superior scholarship. It is also true that Sexton does not unduly offend the conventional wisdom. Even the call for outright abolition of intelligence tests will not startle professors who already teach their students to interpret the I.Q. with extreme caution. But the educationist's enthusiasm for this book probably has a more general portent. Sociological wisdom seems to be welcomed most when it (1) deals with critical educational issues, (2) proceeds from humane value perspectives, (3) contains concrete substantive findings, (4) makes modest demands on technical comprehension, and (5) includes explicit or implied proposals for imminent action.

---

[38] *Ibid.*, pp. 267-272.

By these criteria, the schools of Action, Significance, and Science arrange themselves in descending rank order of acceptability. However, educationists may in due time discover that Scientific sociology also contains rich treasure. Brim's review of the literature on the merits of democratic and authoritarian leadership shows how small group theory in sociology bears on this familiar controversy:

> With the qualification that the findings may be true only for certain kinds of educational systems, this group of studies points to several things: that the dominant role prescription for teachers is to be task oriented, though either role ["authoritarian" or "democratic"] is acceptable; that teachers follow this at the expense of expressive considerations; that they gain respect but lose attraction in doing this; that both teacher and student wish more attention were (or could be) given to expressive or social-emotional matters, and finally, that if they do, learning (or task accomplishment) suffers.[39]

Since some desirable educational objectives are correlates of each type of leadership pattern, the teacher is confronted by two choices: he can select from among competing educational goals and behave accordingly or he can try to convert himself into part authoritarian and part democrat. The first of these alternatives seems clearly unacceptable because, to cite one reason, teachers hope to earn both the respect and affection of their students. Therefore, the teacher would do better to explore the possibility that the second solution can, in fact, be achieved.

The work of Robert F. Bales and his associates at the Harvard Social Relations Laboratory shows that in successful task-oriented groups two distinctive leadership roles ordinarily emerge: an "instrumental" leader

[39] Brim, *op. cit.*, p. 49.

who deals with the technical tasks assigned to the group and an "expressive" leader who is skilled in meeting social-emotional needs and achieving tension reduction. The disturbing finding is that one person can seldom, if ever, perform both roles with equal facility and that the instrumental leader tends to be more respected and the expressive leader better liked.

These findings have obvious implications for experimentation in educational theory and practice. They suggest, for example, that in existing teaching and administrative dyads (say, principal and vice-principal, drama coach and singing coach) one person could be primarily responsible for the instrumental task of the organization while the other should primarily carry out its expressive functions. It might also be desirable to experiment with team-teaching as one possible device for implementing two sets of desirable educational goals.

It would be possible to continue multiplying examples of sociology's potential contribution to education. The sociologist's role as researcher with its component elements of specialist, producer, and originator could be part of a symmetrical relationship whose other half is the educationist as generalist, consumer, and translator. Yet, in point of fact, sociology has had relatively little influence on the conventional wisdom of education. One reason is that the communication gap between specialist and generalist has been further aggravated by physical and social distance. Faculty seminars, joint teaching, conferences, and informal meetings might serve as vehicles for continuous sociological instruction. There is probably no other way that the educational generalist can be introduced to the pertinent professional literature. He is undoubtedly familiar with *The Authoritarian Personality* but not with

Hyman and Sheatsley's critique; he has read Philip
Jacob, but not Allen Barton; and if he has never heard
of Goldhamer and Marshall he cannot test his own
notions of mental health against their findings.[40]

The danger is that the status system of the university
may lead both sociologist and educationist to resist
intellectual desegregation. On some campuses, the
Arts and Sciences faculty clearly regards scholarly exchange with the School of Education as a breach of
academic propriety. The classic problem of culture
contact between persons representing high status and
low status groups thus becomes directly relevant. At
the risk of theoretical over-extension, I quote from a
study of the adjustment of Indian students to the
United States:

> [Contact between high-status and low-status peo-
> ples] impels the visitor to reappraise his own culture
> appreciatively and is usually marked by a heightened
> identification with his own country and an increased
> sensitivity to its status. Very early in his visit the
> Indian student perceives an American image of India
> which contains elements appearing to him to imply
> low status for his home country and by extension for
> him. . . . The ascription of low status implies hos-
> tility which, in turn, evokes reactive hostility. . . . For
> amity, contact is not enough, especially if protracted

[40] T. W. Adorno, Else Frenkel-Brunswik, D. J. Levinson, and
R. N. Sanford, *The Authoritarian Personality,* Harper, 1950;
Herbert H. Hyman and Paul B. Sheatsley, "The Authoritarian
Personality—a Methodological Critique," Richard Christie and
Marie Jahoda, eds., *Studies in the Scope and Method of the
Authoritarian Personality,* The Free Press, 1954, pp. 50-122;
Philip E. Jacob, *Changing Values in College,* Harper, 1957;
Allen N. Barton, *Studying the Effects of College Education,*
Edward H. Hazen Foundation, 1959; Herbert Goldhamer and
Andrew Marshall, *Psychosis and Civilization,* The Free Press,
1953.

contact serves only to accumulate a series of assaults on the self-esteem of nationals of low-status countries.[41]

The sociologist has been given no warrant to play the academic social worker ministering to the intellectually deprived. There is much to deplore in the conventional wisdom of education but also much that is admirable. The territory separating, say, Robert M. Hutchins and the defenders of the *status quo* is wide and within these generous boundaries there is much room for useful maneuver. But the educationist is not engaged in a conspiracy against the mind and he deserves more than academic censure.

It will be interesting to observe how rapidly and to what extent sociology will modify the conventional wisdom of education. Much will depend on how well the educationist's present intellectual apparatus serves him as he confronts the choices of the sixties. For as Galbraith has noted, "The enemy of the conventional wisdom is not ideas but the march of events. . . . The fatal blow to the conventional wisdom comes when the conventional ideas fail signally to deal with some contingency to which obsolescence has made them palpably inapplicable." [42]

[41] Richard D. Lambert and Marvin Bressler, *Indian Students on an American Campus*, University of Minnesota Press, 1956, Chapter 5.
[42] Galbraith, *op. cit.*, pp. 13-14.

# (5)

# *Popular Sociology*

# ELY CHINOY

Sociologists have always devoted a good deal of effort, for reasons that are quite familiar, to defining the distinctive character of their discipline. In seeking to establish their intellectual identity they have found it necessary to distinguish their perspectives from those of other disciplines and to clarify the difference between systematic, tested knowledge and the common-sense understanding that most people necessarily have about the society in which they live.

## TYPES OF POPULAR SOCIOLOGY

In recent years the legitimacy and value of a scientific sociology have been in some measure challenged and cast in doubt by the emergence of a "popular sociology" that deals with many of the same questions that concern social scientists but that is unconstrained by scholarly canons and is explicitly directed toward a "popular" or mass audience. No single formula encompasses the various kinds of description and analysis found in this new product of a generally literate mass society, although they all fall somewhere between journalism and scholarly writing. One major type, which has been identified by *The New Yorker* as the "Russell Lynes school of social anthropology," merely tries to describe or analyze some aspect of American society or culture without benefit of the techniques or accumulated knowledge of academic sociology—or of any other discipline. Among the better known examples of this type of inquiry are Russell Lynes' *A Surfeit of Honey,* A. C. Spectorsky's *The Exurbanites,* and John Keats' *The Crack in the Picture Window.* In a review of *The Exurbanites,* Phyllis McGinley, herself an occasional and knowledgeable practitioner of popular sociology, describes this genre as follows:

> One doesn't have to be Margaret Mead any longer to handle the tools of the anthropologist. One simply goes to live for a while among the tribes of Hollywood, say, or in the wilds of Central Park West. Given a quick ear, a seeing eye, and a convenient notebook, it isn't long before any author worth his salt can emerge with material for a best-seller. It can be scandalous, touching, funny, revealing, or heroic— but it is almost never dull. For to the shock-value of recognition it will add the titillation-value of village gossip. And if the author, like every good historian, writes with a bias, his book is likely to get (and deserve) critical attention. . . . Read as a serious study this book is both disturbing and misleading. Read as fiction it is enormously entertaining.[1]

A second type, best exemplified by Vance Packard's *The Status Seekers* and his more recent *The Pyramid Climbers,* uses the results of scientific research along with other data in order to present an interpretation of some contemporary social or cultural problem. The

[1] *New York Times Book Review,* October 30, 1955, p. 4.

claims of such books rest upon the findings of scholarly research and the independent (and usually less rigorous) inquiries of the writer. *The Status Seekers,* Packard reports, brings together the findings of more than 150 sociologists and other "students of the social scene" as well as the results of eight of his own investigations. The author of *The Pyramid Climbers* examined "a vast number of published and unpublished studies" together with enough interviews of executives and those who select, train, evaluate, and study them to fill "167 stenographic notebooks." Other writers, notably Stuart Chase in *The Proper Study of Mankind* and Selma Hirsh in her summary and interpretation of *The Authoritarian Personality* and other studies of prejudice,[2] have tried to present the findings of social science to a non-academic audience. These latter efforts at popularization carefully report and evaluate the results of scholarly inquiry. In contrast, most popular sociology appears to be more concerned with the audience than the subject matter, more intent on presenting a thesis and an array of facts that will attract a large number of readers than on the careful examination of the validity, consistency, and implications of the results of scientific research.

A third variety of popular sociology is found in the writing of such social critics as Paul Goodman and Dwight Macdonald. Although their interpretations of the ills of modern society usually rest upon their own observations, they frequently use or report the results of scientific investigations. Characteristically, however, they claim for themselves greater insight than they allow among the professional, academic social scientists.

---

[2] Selma Hirsh, *The Fears Men Live By,* Harper, 1955.

## AMERICAN INTROSPECTION

In some respects popular sociology is simply another manifestation of a recurrent American cultural pattern. Americans, it has often been asserted, have an unusual penchant for self-examination. James Bryce begins *The American Commonwealth* by noting the tendency of Americans to inquire of the foreign visitor his view of their institutions. Bryce's own observations and those of Tocqueville, Mrs. Trollope, Harriet Martineau, and a host of others have been carefully and eagerly perused. American historians, philosophers, novelists, critics, journalists, and sociologists have continually engaged in this national intellectual sport. No other country appears to have welcomed so readily public opinion polls, social surveys, and a continual flow of books and articles anatomizing its culture, character, and social organization.

This chronic self-examination stemmed, at least in its origin and for most of the nineteenth century, from the uncertainties of a nation not quite sure of its own identity and often defensive in relation to the more traditional societies of Europe. Ethnic and religious diversity, a fluid social structure, the changes inherent in industrialization and urbanization, and the emergence of America as a world power have sustained this pattern of national introspection. The further transformation of American society and the continual development of new patterns of behavior have kept alive the search for both a personal and a collective identity.

That the contemporary analysis and interpretation of American society, culture, and character should increasingly take a more or less explicit sociological form reflects the rising prestige of the academic discipline and the growing acceptance of the sociological perspective as a useful instrument in understanding significant features of the modern world. Two distinguished sociologists as different in many of their views as Talcott Parsons and the late C. Wright Mills have recently asserted that we are entering a period dominated by a sociological perspective. "We may say," notes Parsons, "that, ideologically, a 'sociological' era has begun to emerge, following an 'economic' and, more recently, a 'psychological' era." [3] "The sociological imagination," Mills asserted, "is becoming the major common denominator of our cultural life and its signal feature." [4] These views, of course, may be challenged as the exaggerated judgments of self-interested observers. Sociology, after all, is still déclassé among many scholars in more traditional fields, and there remains persistent hostility to the sociological enterprise in some quarters—witness Justice William O. Douglas's comment: "Our plague these days are the sociologists who, like Madison Avenue, classify people and things, putting everyone and everything into neat categories." [5] But sociology is no longer widely looked upon, as it once was, as consisting merely of the study of crime, delinquency, slums, and other social problems, or, alternatively, as a presumptuous newcomer trying to encompass in exceedingly abstract theories everything "social." The usefulness of its categories is gaining wide recognition, and its methods and theories have become sufficiently reputable to warrant the flattery of imitation and application by popular writers

---

[3] "Some Problems Confronting Sociology as a Profession," *American Sociological Review*, 24 (August, 1959), p. 553.
[4] *The Sociological Imagination*, Oxford University Press, 1959, p. 14.
[5] Review of Oscar and Mary Handlin, *The Dimensions of Liberty*, *New York Times Book Review*, October 22, 1961, p. 36.

as well as by scholars in other fields—even if sometimes to the accompaniment of open skepticism or
outright denial of the claims of sociology and its
practitioners.

## SOCIOLOGISTS WITHOUT PORTFOLIO

Much of this implicit flattery, however, is viewed
critically by social scientists who see in most popular
sociology many of the intellectual characteristics
against which they have long had to contend. Modern
social science emerged in part as a reaction against
the kind of unsystematic observation and uncontrolled
speculation found today in the work of Lynes, Spectorsky, Macdonald, Goodman, and others. It has tried to
replace casual, albeit sometimes acute, observation
with carefully collected, reliable data, and to subject
speculation to logical and empirical tests. Sociologists,
therefore, have found little of value in most popular
sociology. When they have not ignored it, they have
usually roundly and, on the whole, justifiably attacked
it.

The work of the "anthropologists without portfolio,"
as Irwin Edman once described these non-professional
social observers, abounds in seemingly perceptive generalizations the meaning and validity of which often
become questionable when subjected to careful scru-
tiny. Men, Russell Lynes tells us in *A Surfeit of Honey*,
have become the "new servant class," the tenders of
mechanized household equipment, masters of the
barbecue, do-it-yourselfers who have replaced the
hired help. What it means sociologically to identify
husbands as servants (other than to dangle a catchy
phrase before a popular audience) and to what extent
and among which groups this change has occurred are
never spelled out. Documentation consists chiefly of

example and inference: "Recently a friend of mine told me of a telephone conversation he had had . . ." (p. 50). "As more and more women took full-time and part-time jobs, more and more mechanical gadgets were invented to lighten the burdens of housework. Someone, however, had to help run the gadgets . . ." (p. 55). The only "hard" data to support Lynes's generalizations are taken from public opinion polls. One of these polls reports that "62 per cent of American husbands are intimate with dishwater." No questions are raised about how often, under what conditions, or in what kinds of families this intimacy occurs, although it seems obvious, as the data secured by several family sociologists show, that the extent of male participation in household tasks varies widely and is clearly related to specific features of family life.

In trying to make available to a mass audience the results of scholarly research, the popular sociologist is often guilty of distorting the available data and providing a misleading picture of both contemporary society and the findings of sociological inquiry. Eric Larrabee, one of the most able non-professional observers of modern society, points out that "in the process of converting [sociological facts and terminology] to layman's language, many of the reservations and caveats get lost; and the results are subsequently served up to the public with a spurious and unintended authority, as the pronouncements of social science." [6] Vance Packard's *The Status Seekers* provides a glaring example of the errors and over-simplification to which popularization oriented to a mass audience can lead. Historical contrasts are exaggerated; it is not true, for example, as Packard claims, that "social scientists, until a few years ago [seemingly prior to about 1940],

[6] Eric Larrabee, *The Self-Conscious Society*, Doubleday, 1960, p. 35.

knew more about the social classes of New Guinea than they did of those in the United States of America" (p. 4).[7] Differences among sociologists as to the meaning and validity of various data are disregarded. W. Lloyd Warner, writes Packard, "after assessing his findings and comparing them with other findings, concluded that there is at least something of Jonesville in all American communities" (p. 26). No reference is made to the sharp criticism by other sociologists of Warner's conclusion about how typical Jonesville, a relatively small midwestern community, actually was. Difficulties in interpreting the available data are never mentioned, and in some instances, important studies are disregarded. Packard ignores, for example, the fact that the amount of social mobility found by any investigator will depend to some extent upon the number of classes into which he divides the sample or population he is studying. No mention is made, in the analysis of social mobility, of the work of Natalie Rogoff, whose conclusions, it should be added, raise some questions about Packard's interpretation. Finally, no discrimination is made among different kinds of data: an interview with an appliance salesman about wages, reports from building contractors, and results of a national survey are seemingly given equal weight.

As one might expect, however, this type of academic criticism seems to have little effect upon public interest in non-academic sociology. Perhaps the most striking example of scholarly rejection and popular acceptance is *The Status Seekers*, which was not reviewed in most academic journals. Those social scientists who did review it were extremely critical; Raymond J. Murphy, for example, writing in the *American Anthropologist*, accused the author of misstatement, ignorance, misinterpretation, and the expression of directly contradic-

---

[7] All quotations from the Pocket Book edition, 1961.

tory values.[8] Reviews in most newspapers and magazines, on the other hand, were generally very favorable, although the book received only brief and critical comment in *Time, The Atlantic Monthly,* and *The New Yorker.* (Interestingly enough, the reviewers in *The New York Times Book Review* and the *Saturday Review of Literature,* Cleveland Amory and A. C. Spectorsky, respectively, are themselves popular sociologists.) Within two weeks of publication *The Status Seekers* made the *New York Times* best seller list where it remained for fifty-two weeks, one third of that period in first place.

Although their contribution to the understanding of modern society and their usefulness to the sociologist are limited—or even on occasion questionable—these non-academic interpretations and descriptions cannot be ignored by the student of society and culture. Not only do they constitute an interesting and perhaps important cultural phenomenon and a challenge to the more careful and systematic efforts of social scientists, but they also raise significant questions about the nature and functions of contemporary sociology.

## WHY IS IT POPULAR?

The vogue of popular sociology, despite its readily demonstrated limitations, indicates in part simply the authors' knowledge of those aspects of sociological inquiry likely to appeal to a large public. Most of the books and articles contained in this genre are devoted to the description and analysis of status distinctions, life styles, and social mobility. The point of departure is often an apparent discrepancy between prevailing values and beliefs and the realities of social life—

---

[8] *American Authropologist,* 61 (December, 1959), pp. 1157-1159.

between equalitarianism on the one hand and invidious social distinctions and limitations on equal opportunity on the other (*The Status Seekers*), between an individualistic ethos and the coerciveness and paternalism of the large corporation (Alan Harrington's *Life in the Crystal Palace*), between the optimism of an affluent society and the problems created by *A Surfeit of Honey*, between the presumed desirability of owning one's home and the difficulties inherent in the new suburban subdivisions (*The Crack in the Picture Window*). These books thus combine reporting of the rich and intimate details of daily life with a discussion of important problems faced by many Americans.

Concern with status and mobility, of course, is hardly new in American culture. Lacking clear social distinctions and without a firm and widely recognized system of ranks, American society has long appeared to be not merely open and fluid, but even amorphous and without recognizable order and structure other than that imposed by law and formal organization. Many writers—scholars, social critics, novelists, and journalists—have tried to identify both the prevailing values and the ordered system of relationships to be found in this seemingly free-wheeling, equalitarian society. Tocqueville and Veblen, the sociological "Fathers" (for example Ward, Sumner, Ross, and Cooley, who, as Charles Page has shown,[9] dealt at length with problems of class), and the novelists Edith Wharton, William Dean Howells, and Theodore Dreiser, to name but a few, have explored the nature and influence of invidious social distinctions and the consequences of mobility and social striving.

What is new in this recent non-academic interest in status and its concomitants, in addition to the fact that it masquerades as sociology or draws upon schol-

---
[9] Charles H. Page, *Class and American Sociology*, Dial, 1940.

arly research, is the tendency to deprecate economic differences and to ignore the political aspects of status. Edith Wharton, for example, who portrayed so acutely the values and life styles of the old upper class and the new, saw clearly the constant tension between wealth and "breeding." The novel, Lionel Trilling has observed, always deals with manners *and* money, with status *and* class. The attention of popular sociologists (and, unfortunately, of many academic sociologists too, it should be noted) is focused almost solely upon invidious ranking and status striving, defined chiefly in terms of manners, consumption patterns, and inter-personal relations. Packard, for instance, cites approvingly the conclusion of the research director of the *Chicago Tribune* that "our consuming and spending habits equal our position in the social-class structure." [10] This narrowing of perspective reflects the relative affluence of the United States since World War II and the apparent muting of harsh economic and political conflict. With most Americans sharing the fruits of a highly productive technology, their anxieties center more upon the status value of their acquisitions and actions, and less upon the economic and political meaning of their behavior.

Such books as *The Status Seekers, The Exurbanites, A Surfeit of Honey,* and *The Crack in the Picture Window* exploit these anxieties. Although ostensibly critical of the values and behavior they describe, most authors of popular sociology avoid any sharp collision with existing standards and institutions. (Paul Goodman and Dwight Macdonald are notable exceptions.) If they merely describe, albeit with a bias and bite that may draw blood from their victims, they are likely, in the end, to offer some comforting reassurance that, in spite of everything, things are not as bad as they

---

[10] *The Status Seekers,* p. 48.

seem. Thus Spectorsky, after describing "briskly and busily and bloodily" the physical, psychic, and social strains to which exurbanites are subject, concludes: "And not only do they do the best they can at the difficult and exciting job of living, but the job they do is, under the circumstances, often remarkably good." [11] If these authors do offer some solution to the problems they explore, they are likely to confine themselves to moral exhortation and the reiteration of conventional platitudes. After devoting most of *The Status Seekers* to depicting both the obstacles to social mobility and the endless manifestations of status striving, Packard concludes: "I think we should all be happier and live more stimulating lives if . . . we judged people not by the symbols they display but rather by their individual worth. . . . while becoming practicing individualists we should work to make opportunity a reality in our land of the free" (p. 316).

Packard's most recent volume, *The Pyramid Climbers,*[12] displays even more clearly the combination of a seemingly critical exposé—in this case of the "sanity" of "the mechanics of success in the modern corporation"—with tips on how to succeed and some reassurance that things are likely to improve. The analysis of the prerequisites and channels for success in the great corporate hierarchies focuses upon the "isolating, dehumanizing, deindividualizing, and manipulating" experiences to which aspiring executives are subject. Yet criticism is suspended when the author provides a list of "seven abilities that seem to count greatly." While not offered as "a guaranteed recipe for success," Packard archly observes: "If an ambitious young manager wishes to tuck it under his pillow for a nightly reminder, however, I am sure it will not do him any

---

[11] *The Exurbanites,* Berkley edition, p. 251
[12] McGraw-Hill, 1962.

harm" (p. 155). The thrust of the criticism contained in most of the book is further softened by a concluding discussion of the efforts being made by a few men to create a "philosophy of management" that might "make the individual manager in the corporate hierarchy a more independent, mature, self-controlling, and committed person."

It is perhaps inevitable that interpretations of modern culture and society designed for a mass audience will avoid any sharp conflict with the values of potential readers. By focusing on real tensions and by seeming to expose the pretentious, spurious, and apparently hypocritical, they attract an audience. If they implicitly —or explicitly—offer hints on how to achieve conventional values, even as they appear to question them, so much the better. By finally reaffirming these values and avoiding any serious challenge to established institutions they manage not to alienate most of their prospective readers.

## THE UNINTENDED CONTRIBUTION
## OF SOCIOLOGY

Paradoxically, the success of popular sociology is due not only to the growing acceptability and reputability of the sociological perspective, but also to the limitations of academic research and writing. There is, perhaps inevitably in an increasingly specialized society, a gap between specialists in different fields as well as between scholars and even educated laymen. When the separation is too great, popularizers of various kinds are likely to fill the breach. Unfortunately, many professional sociologists have needlessly widened the gap between themselves and both other scholars and their potential non-academic audience. They have reinforced the persisting animus toward their efforts by an awkward and pretentious intellectual style too often marked by academic ritualism and a crude scientism.

Intellectual style, which is sometimes reduced by both critics and defenders of sociology to a matter merely of jargon, refers to the general mode of expression.[13] Many sociologists, of course, deny that it has any relevance to their scientific work, but as long as they cannot present their findings and interpretations in purely mathematical form—a goal pursued by some—they cannot avoid problems of style. Just as there is some truth in the old saying that clothes make the man, so is there some justification for the view that how men express their ideas is often significantly related to the substance of their thought. An impoverished style often bespeaks a limited mind, although embellishments of style do not necessarily betoken either knowledge or understanding.

Despite some notable exceptions,* sociologists have developed in recent years a style that repels many other scholars and many well-educated laymen. Much sociological writing, particularly in the professional journals, manages to present relatively simple facts and ideas in awkward, complex, and laborious prose. After editing the *American Sociological Review* for three years, Charles Page, in his final report to the American Sociological Association, stressed his conviction "that painstaking formulation should be an important part of scholarly craftsmanship";[14] in a later unpublished

---

[13] This discussion of intellectual style draws heavily upon Charles H. Page, "Sociologists as Craftsmen in Communication," an unpublished lecture delivered at the University of Pennsylvania, December 11, 1961.

* Several of these exceptions are listed by Robert Bierstedt in Chapter 2—EDITOR.

[14] "Report of the Editor of the *American Sociological Review*," *American Sociological Review*, 25 (December, 1960), pp. 940-942.

paper, he noted that "sociological writing too frequently gives the impression that sociologists are insensitive to the norms of syntax and suffer from limited vocabularies." Neglect of synonyms and antonyms, a widespread preference for big words and long phrases, and the use of technical language even when conventional expressions would be adequate contribute to this impression.

Crude and pretentious language is frequently linked with the absence of a sense of proportion in matters of substance. Sociologists are often accused, correctly, of documenting or demonstrating the obvious. From a scientific point of view there is nothing wrong with this; what is taken as obvious is sometimes incorrect. It is often necessary to confirm the commonplace. The defect lies in reporting in portentous terms and with a breathless air of discovery—and this is a matter of style—what everyone has always assumed to be true.

As in the case of many other scholars, sociologists are prone to academic fads and rituals that often become part of their intellectual style. Sociological studies often suffer from excessive footnoting, the prefacing of limited research reports with what in many cases are unnecessary and irrelevant theoretical statements, citation of major writers on obvious points, and all too frequent redefinition of terms the meaning of which is now generally accepted. These practices contribute to an image of the professional sociologist as one who knows only the obvious—and then insists upon describing it in unnecessarily abstract and wordy fashion.

Sociologists often defend themselves against these criticisms of their intellectual style on ostensibly scientific grounds—the need for precision, the limitations of our ordinary vocabulary, the novelty of their ideas, the importance of linking theory and empirical research, the scientific irrelevance of a concern with the niceties of expression. These defenses obviously have some validity. Empirical findings may have important implications for abstract theory, and a technical vocabulary is frequently necessary in order to be precise, to avoid the connotations of familiar words, and to make new distinctions and express original ideas. But in all too many instances these defenses conceal a crude scientism—the spurious or excessive application of the criteria or methods of science. In their search for reliable data rather than casual observation many sociologists welcome any systematically gained facts, however trivial, and ignore other useful sources of information. In an effort to establish their scientific standing, often questioned by both natural scientists and scholars in the humanities, sociologists sometimes make an elaborate and unnecessary display of research procedures in studies of only limited substantive content—a kind of conspicuous flexing of their scientific muscles. In their search for reliable data rather than casual observation they are apt to welcome any systematically gained facts, however trivial, and ignore other useful sources of information. The undeniable achievements of sociology have become grounds for a professional provincialism that denies the possibility that non-professionals can contribute to the systematic understanding of society and culture.

Sociological description, analysis, and interpretation are to be found in the work of many writers who are not professional sociologists—journalists, creative writers who portray with an artist's eye the realities of social life, and other scholars such as historians, economists, and political scientists. These sources retain some value for the professional; they may provide useful observation, historical depth, a sense of the significant, or suggestive hypotheses to be tested in systematic research. Occasionally they may even stand, as they are, as useful contributions. There are those who think that some of our best contemporary sociology is contained in the work of men such as the historian Richard Hofstadter, the political scientist Edward Banfield, and the journalist William H. Whyte, Jr. Yet, as the professional sociologist has extended his research skills, elaborated more complex theoretical schemes, and accumulated a growing body of reliable data, he has tended more and more to separate his endeavors from those of the non-professional student of society and to disregard or deprecate publications that do not possess appropriate professional and therefore presumably scientific accreditation.

There are many exceptions to these generalizations and one might argue that it is both unnecessary and ungracious to speak of these things; the scorner's seat is easily filled. Much of the criticism that is leveled against sociology can be leveled against many other fields. Many critics of sociological style, after all, have buttressed their complaints by implicitly comparing the worst in sociology with the best in other fields. Yet the defects of style and, correlatively, of judgment among sociologists are, in my opinion, sufficiently widespread to lend a substantial validity to many of the complaints leveled against them. Much of the potential public for serious sociological inquiry, alienated by these oppressive qualities, has welcomed the cheaper and often shoddy merchandise of the casual journalist or unqualified popularizer.

In their pursuit of scientific excellence, many of the sociologists who ignore—or even justify—these deficiencies appear to be little concerned with their failure to communicate outside the professional fraternity. In addition to denying that sociological craftsmanship includes the ability to communicate clearly, economically, and effectively the results of their inquiries, they avoid the task of making their findings widely known. In view of the rising interest in sociological questions and the growing repute of sociology as a discipline, this abdication of responsibility leaves a large and growing field to less qualified writers.

Lack of interest in reaching the non-professional audience reflects both the general drift of research interest in recent years and what seems to be a changing conception of the functions of sociology. Increasingly, it appears, sociological inquiry is directed toward problems facing the administrator, the manager, the professional—business executives, doctors, lawyers, social workers, educators, military men. The newest major area of research interest, medical sociology, for example, has concentrated on problems of interest chiefly to medical educators, hospital administrators, and (some) practicing physicians. Sociologists are now in demand in business schools, hospitals, schools of social work, law schools, and in many large organizations, both public and private, as purveyors of information and consultants on policy and procedure.

As the relevant publics for research become more limited, it becomes less important for sociologists to concern themselves with the larger audience. When professionals become specialists who can aid the "social practitioner," to use Hans Zetterberg's phrase (as though everyone is not, in a sense, a social practitioner), they can in fact disregard other potential publics that might be interested in their studies.[15] They need to communicate, then, only with their clients and their professional colleagues. Indeed, maintenance of a reasonable level of jargon and incompre-

---

[15] See Hans L. Zetterberg, *Social Theory and Social Practice,* Bedminster Press, 1962.

hensibility may even enhance in the eyes of actual or potential clients both the "mysteries" of the discipline and the scientific aura surrounding it.

A considerable amount of sociological literature, of course, will inevitably be directed toward other professionals, and undoubtedly a good deal of sociological research will always be of interest only to limited publics. It can hardly be otherwise. But sociology has always pursued a greater goal too, the enlargement of men's understanding and of their ability to control their own fate. A recent report of the Behavioral Sciences Subpanel of the President's Scientific Advisory Committee notes that

> . . . at a deeper level [the behavioral sciences] are changing the conception of human nature—our fundamental ideas about human desires and human possibilities. When such conceptions change, society changes. . . . The casual way in which unproved behavioral hypotheses often find widespread acceptance underscores the importance of strengthening and deepening the behavioral sciences and of securing better public understanding of what they are and what they are not.[16]

If sociologists confine their energies to narrowly defined problems and fail to make available or understandable to other scholars and to educated laymen those facts and theories of interest to the non-professional, they should hardly be surprised if other and often less competent persons fill the breach. If sociologists do not wish to see their work by-passed or distorted by authors of the popular sociology to which they properly object, then they must seek to remedy

---

[16] "Strengthening the Behavioral Sciences," Report of the Behavioral Sciences Subpanel of the President's Scientific Advisory Committee, *Science*, 136 (April, 1962), p. 233.

the deficiencies of style that stimulate ersatz substitutes, and they must be willing to assume at least some of the responsibility for disseminating to the wider public the more significant results of their investigations.

# Selected Readings

American Council of Learned Societies and the National Council for the Social Studies, *The Social Studies and the Social Sciences*. New York: Harcourt, Brace & World, Inc., 1962. These seven essays treat the present status and potential role of the social sciences in secondary education, matters briefly discussed in Chapters 1 and 4 of the present volume. See especially "Introduction" (pp. 3-19) by Bernard Berelson and "Sociology" (pp. 156-170) by Gresham M. Sykes.

Barzun, Jacques, *The House of Intellect*. New York: Harper & Row, 1959. In this lively treatment of what he depicts as a serious decline of intellect in the United States, Mr. Barzun, teacher and university administrator, presents a frequently insightful and sometimes exasperating discussion of teachers and the academic world which includes a sharp critique of sociologists and educators.

Berelson, Bernard, *Graduate Education in the United States*. New York: McGraw-Hill Book Company, Inc., 1960. This generally excellent assessment of graduate education, based upon extensive study, contains both factual information and opinion that are directly relevant to issues presented in Chapters 1 and 3 of the present volume, including the question of appropriate training of future teachers.

Brim, Orville G., Jr., *Sociology and the Field of Education.* New York: Russell Sage Foundation, 1958. This "bulletin" prepared for the American Sociological Association, is a succinct, systematic, and lucid review of sociological studies of educational institutions and a highly useful directive for needed research in this previously largely neglected field; it should be read by anyone interested in the relationship between education and sociology.

Caplow, Theodore, and McGee, Reece J., *The Academic Marketplace.* New York: Basic Books, Inc., 1958. Here is empirical documentation of the high priority of the "publish or perish" criterion and the decline of teaching prowess as an important consideration in the recruitment and career mobility of academic men —a theme discussed in Chapter 3 of the present volume. But this readable and frequently witty book also is an insightful introduction to the structure and culture of American colleges.

Clark, Burton R., *The Open Door College: A Case Study.* New York: McGraw-Hill Book Company, Inc., 1960. An excellent detailed study of the administration, student makeup and "traffic," and, to some extent, teaching problems in a public junior college—an illustration of the "centers of mass education" discussed in Chapter 1 of the present volume.

Halsey, A. H., Floud, Jean, and Anderson, C. Arnold, editors, *Education, Economy, and Society: A Reader in the Sociology of Education.* New York: The Free Press of Glencoe, 1961. A large collection of empirical studies and essays, drawn from British, American, and other Western sources, concerned with formal schooling and economic change, shifting patterns of social mobility, educational selection and achievement, changing social functions of schools, and the role of the teacher in this dynamic setting.

Lazarsfeld, Paul F., and Thielens, Wagner, Jr., with a Field Report by David Riesman, *The Academic Mind: Social Scientists in a Time of Crisis.* Glencoe: The

Free Press, 1958. Although peripheral to the themes discussed in the present volume, this first major empirical study of the impact of political conditions (during the McCarthy Era) upon teachers and teaching (in the social sciences) provides highly useful information about academic men and their vulnerabilities and strengths in different types of colleges and universities in the United States.

Merton, Robert K., Broom, Leonard, and Cottrell, Leonard S., Jr., editors, *Sociology Today: Problems and Prospects.* New York: Basic Books, Inc., 1959. Chapter 5, "The Sociology of Education" by Neal Gross, is a summary and assessment of much of the research in this "relatively underdeveloped and unfashionable subfield of sociology." Chapter 25, "Sociology as a Teaching Enterprise" by Charles H. Page, discusses "sociological imperialism," the scientific, humanistic, and reformistic components of sociology, the latter's "marginality," and the relations of sociology to other social sciences in the teaching setting.

Riesman, David, *Constraint and Variety in American Education.* Lincoln: University of Nebraska Press, 1956. An insightful and frequently provocative discussion of educational patterns and trends in both the colleges and secondary schools, with particular emphasis on the "newer" social sciences of anthropology, sociology, and social psychology—required reading for all educators and academic men.

Rosenberg, Bernard, and White, David Manning, editors, *Mass Culture: The Popular Arts in America.* Glencoe: The Free Press, 1957. The educational implications of "Popular Sociology," the subject of Chapter 5 of the present volume (and also discussed in Chapter 1), have received very little scholarly attention. For diverse interpretations of the sources and intellectual consequences of popular culture—of which popular sociology seems to be a variety—see the selections in this reader by Bernard Rosenberg (pp. 3-12), David M. White (pp. 13-21), Alexis de Tocqueville (pp. 27-34), Jose Ortega y Gasset (pp. 41-45), Dwight Macdonald (pp. 59-73), Irving Howe (pp. 496-503), Ernest Van den Haag (pp. 504-536), and Melvin Tumin (pp. 548-556).

Sanford, Nevitt, editor, *The American College: A Psychological and Social Interpretation of the Higher Learning.* New York: John Wiley & Sons, Inc., 1962. Together, the twenty-nine chapters of this impressive book, many of them based upon systematic empirical research, constitute the first large-scale social science analysis of higher education in this country. With reference to the present volume, see especially Chapter 1, "Higher Education as a Social Problem" by Nevitt Sanford; Chapter 3, "The Viability of the American College" by David Riesman and Christopher Jencks; Chapter 7, "Changing Functions of the College Professor" by Robert Knapp; Chapter 26, "The Place of Higher Education in a Changing Society" by Campbell Stewart; and Chapter 29, "Research and Policy in Higher Education" by Nevitt Sanford.

Sibley, Elbridge, *The Education of Sociologists in the United States.* New York: Russell Sage Foundation, 1963. This report and evaluation of the training of sociologists, based upon an extensive and intensive three-year study, was not available until after this book went to press. See particularly Chapter 2, "Summary of Findings and Recommendations"; Chapter 3, Number of Sociologists and Their Occupations"; Chapter 4, "The Graduate Schools"; Chapter 5, "The Students: Aptitude, Motivation, and Educational Background"; Chapter 8, "Content of Graduate Training"; and Chapter 9, "Graduates' Appraisal and Criticism of Their Own Training."

Znaniecki, Florian, *The Social Role of the Man of Knowledge.* New York: Columbia University Press, 1940. This short book continues to be unsurpassed as a theoretical discussion of the principal types, functions, and subroles of men of knowledge: scholars or schoolmen, technologists, sages, and creators or explorers.

For readers wishing to learn more about the sociological enterprise and its perspectives, there is of course a large and growing literature. Four quite different introductions to this subject are presented in the following volumes: Ely Chinoy, *Society: An Introduction to Sociology* (New York: Random House, 1961), a systematic general textbook; Robert K. Merton *et al.*, editors, *Sociology Today* (cited above), which contains highly informed discussions of most specializations in this many-sided field; Peter L. Berger, *Invitation to Sociology: A Humanistic Perspective* (Garden City: Doubleday Anchor Books, 1963), a stimulating and lucid essay on different sociological perspectives, the contributions of major sociologists, sociology's interconnections with other disciplines, and its influence upon individuals as a "form of consciousness"; William Bruce Cameron, *Informal Sociology: A Casual Introduction to Sociological Thinking* (New York: a Random House Study in Sociology, 1963), a dozen light-hearted but basically serious essays on such diverse matters of sociological concern as statistical analysis, group formation, humor, social mobility, jazz music, and the influence of college architecture upon education.